A Once in a Lifetime Adventure to Meet the Best Coaches in College Hoops

andrew hemminger

dave bensch

Oak Town United, LLC
Oak Harbor, Ohio

ISBN 13: 978-0-615-15947-8
ISBN 10: 0-615-15947-8

Printed in the United States of America

Oak Town United, LLC
Oak Harbor, Ohio

www.destinationbasketball.com
E-mail: dh@destinationbasketball.com

Information was gathered and verified through a number of people and places - including the *Official NCAA Men's Basketball Records Book*, and a number of individual school media guides that were provided to us by each university.

To Mom, Dad, Papa and Grandma
-Andrew

To Mom, Dad, Jeff and my beautiful wife, Mackenzie
Philippians 4:13
-Dave

THE V FOUNDATION®
for Cancer Research

Contents

Acknowledgments

It took a large number of people to make *Destination Basketball* happen, and it never would have gotten off the ground without the support of our families and the instrumental help of three gentlemen:

Jay Bilas,
Howard Schwab
and Grant Cummings

Rick Barnes
John Beilein
Jim Boeheim
Mike Brey
Jim Calhoun
John Chaney
Denny Crum
Jamie Dixon
Billy Donovan
Mark Few
Ben Howland
Tom Izzo
Gene Keady
Mike Krzyzewski

Thad Matta
Lute Olson
Rick Pitino
Skip Prosser
Bo Ryan
Kelvin Sampson
Bill Self
Dean Smith
Tubby Smith
Bruce Weber
Gary Williams
Roy Williams
John Wooden
Jay Wright

Alford, Steve
Andrews, Erin
Bensch, Arlyn & Candy
Bensch, Jeff
Bensch, Mackenzie
Bockbrader, Tom & Mickey
Boyle, Pat
Braithwaite, Bill
Brendlinger, Nancy
Brown, Kent
Buchan, Dean
Burke, Doris
Cafarelli, Bernie
Campbell, J.D.
McCall, Brittany
Coughlin, Kyle
Cowgill, Judy
Cuneen, Jacquelyn
Dakich, Dan
Dalziel, Leslie
Delp, Cleves
Demarest, Fred
Donnelly, Jason
Dougherty, Larry
Edson, Sue
Egelhoff, Dave
Farley, Randy
Finney, Ryan
Fulton, Maureen
Gard, Mike
Gaver, Tony
Groce, John
Haase, Jarod
Hamner, Tracy
Harrity, Mike
Hemminger, Brad & Julie
Hertz, Darren
Hill, Justice
Hoffman, Tami
Holbrook, Jennifer
Hotchkiss, Greg
Jackson, Jon
Jacobs, Melissa
Kay, Frank
Kirkendall, Ruth
Kirschner, Steve
Klein, Kenny
Knopp, Kathy
Larson, Matt
LaValle, Kelly
Lavin, Steve
Lemley, Debra
Leshney, John
McElroy, B.J.
Montgomery, Mark
Moore, Pete
Muncy, Kyle
Nicholson, Lisa
Noggle, Amber
Noggle, Anna
Paige, Richard
Parks, Leslie
Pepelea, Artie
Pierce, Oliver
Radsick, Justin "Sacker"
Roe, Steve
Ryan, Kelly, Will & Matt
Ruple, Kevin
Salituro, Chuck
Schneider, Ray
Sheridan, Mike
Spinazze, Nick
Stone, LaMonta
Stricklin, Scott
Tatum, Vinny
Theisen, Chris
Torres, Larry
Vitale, Dick
Vitale, Sherri
Vuocolo, Christina
Walsh, John
Weight, Erianne
Weinar, Mike
Whitt, Alan
Wiechers, Nate
Yaman, Jason

Special Words from "The Schwab"

Determination. It is a word often used in the world of sports journalism. Underdogs are often credited with determination because they fight hard to accomplish their goal, being successful in their battle to prevail against adversity.

Determination is a word I would use to describe the efforts of Andrew and David. Ever since I first met them during a visit to Bristol, Connecticut to spend a day at ESPN, I knew that the word determination was appropriate in describing the passion and enthusiasm they had over an amazing and complex project.

It was one thing to have a goal of meeting and interviewing so many prominent college basketball coaches. It is another to do so by driving thousands of miles, through most of the 50 states, to get the job done. Now that's determination.

It was an intriguing project because most Division I coaches barely have enough time to say hello to their families. They have to worry about recruiting, about appearances at booster clubs, dealing with issues that involve their current players and staff, and yes, the actual coaching during the season! It is a reflection on Andrew and David that they worked so hard to get so many high-profile coaches to speak with them and reveal their feelings on various topics. It's all about determination.

That's why I am proud to help them in any way with this project. These guys are winners. They set a goal and worked hard to reach it. Fans of college basketball are the other big winners in this story. Enjoy.

Howie Schwab
ESPN's "Stump the Schwab"

Through four seasons on ESPN's "Stump the Schwab", Howie went 64-16 (.800) against the competition from around the country.

Foreword

The best coaches and players often demonstrate passion, commitment and hunger for the game. Louisville coach Rick Pitino has said he wants his players to be "PHD's"....poor, hungry and driven.

In the summer of 2006, I met two young men that exemplified those principles, and it was refreshing. I sat down with Andrew and Dave in Louisville for a short interview. We talked, and took a couple of pictures, and I learned about the journey they were just beginning.

Andrew and Dave were college students that had hatched an idea for a book on college basketball, and were traveling around the country to interview the game's greatest coaches.

On a shoestring budget, they were sleeping in their car and driving countless hours to get to each great coach. I couldn't have been more impressed by their earnest drive and enthusiasm for the game.

This book gives you great insight into the game of college basketball, as seen through the eyes of two of its most passionate and driven fans.

They have lived their dream over the past year, and have worked and sacrificed to make that dream a reality. They have also exemplified what the game is really all about. Do you remember a time when you were that hungry?

Jay Bilas
ESPN College Basketball Analyst

Jay played at Duke from 1982-86, scored 1,062 points and was drafted by Dallas. The '86 team went 37-3 and reached the NCAA Championship game.

1

The Opening Tip

This is the story of two ordinary guys - best friends from the tiny northern Ohio town of Oak Harbor - and the simple idea that led us on a 15-month adventure from coast-to-coast to meet many of the best in college basketball.

Before entering our final year of college (Dave at Baldwin-Wallace and myself at Bowling Green), we decided that we needed to embark on one colossal project before graduating and quite possibly being forced to go our separate ways.

Teammates on the baseball diamond and the basketball court from little league through high school, we concluded that we needed to conduct a project involving college hoops. Although baseball was a slightly different story, neither of us received any offers to continue playing basketball after high school, and rightfully so. However, it never deterred our love for the collegiate game.

On June 14, 2006, the idea became clear. We began devising a list of some of the greatest coaches in the nation - past and present. Dean Smith, Mike Krzyzewski, Rick Pitino, Jim Boeheim, Lute Olson, John Wooden - we shied away from no one. From there, we decided that we wanted to meet, speak with and interview each individual on the 29-coach list in person. No phone calls, written letters, e-mails or faxes - in person only.

Not to ask about a single play, player, game or season but to learn more about their individual style, their philosophies, their methods, their influences, their experiences and their time within basketball.

It was an interesting idea, it was certainly fun to think about the potential experiences, but we possessed nothing more than the idea itself. We didn't know anyone on the "inside" at the powerhouse programs like North Carolina, Kansas, UCLA, UConn, Duke, Florida or Kentucky. All we had was an idea and a willingness to run with it.

The evening of June 14, we scoured the internet looking for any leads we could find that may help us get in touch with the coaches from our list. We sent out nearly two dozen cold e-mails to school sports information directors (SID), secretaries and administrative assistants describing what we were attempting to accomplish.

In each e-mail we asked for a maximum of 15 minutes with the coach and informed each recipient that we were looking for positive information, not the sometimes frequently asked questions from certain members of the media following practice and games.

To our extreme surprise, the following morning yielded a number of e-mails. Several were looking for more information, another was clearly skeptical of our intentions, however, one was very inviting, asking us to call the attached number to set up a date and time. It was from Coach Pitino's camp at the University of Louisville.

Four days later we found ourselves in his office, less than a week after the project's conception. It was unbelievable! From that day forward, June 19, 2006, the idea became a reality and took off.

The following is our 15-month odyssey and how we had the good fortune to spend time with nearly 30 of the best. It depicts what it took for us to get face time with each coach and the actual interview which takes a look into the careers and lives of some of the greatest teachers that sports has to offer.

23

TRIPS

421

DAYS

1,134

PHONE CALLS

2,314

EMAILS

27,125

MILES TRAVELED

13,152

WINS

399

NCAA TOURNAMENTS

80

FINAL FOURS

36

NATIONAL CHAMPIONSHIPS

29

OF THE BEST
IN COLLEGE HOOPS

Rick Pitino
June 19, 2006

Starting this adventure on June 14, 2006, we never anticipated Coach Pitino being our first interview, and we certainly never expected it to come just five days after the project's conception.

For no particular reason, we originally thought that scheduling an interview with Coach Pitino would be very difficult. However, Vinny Tatum, Coach Pitino's executive assistant, penciled us in for 3 p.m on Monday, June 19 while the men's basketball program was putting on a camp for high school athletes.

We were not assured a formal interview as it was to be left up to Coach Pitino to decide how much time he had. However, we thought the small window of opportunity to meet with a coach that has advanced three different schools (Providence, Kentucky and Louisville) to the Final Four was more than worth the 10-hour round-trip.

On the ensuing Monday, we arrived on the Louisville campus just before 1 p.m. and entered the Swain Student Activities Center, which houses the men's basketball offices among many other things. We wanted only to check in and thought that Coach Pitino might have more time for us if we provided a larger window.

Although we expected to wait until our scheduled 3 p.m. appointment, when we spoke to the secretary at the front desk, she promptly called Mr. Tatum who came out to greet us.

He led us down the hallway and we thought that we were headed to his office to chat for a few minutes. But we soon passed his space and before we knew it we were shaking hands with Coach Pitino himself who came from behind his desk to meet us in the middle of his palatial estate-type office.

It was the first coach's office that we had seen and it didn't disappoint. Among the vast number of pictures and autographed mementos, one of the most unique features was a large window that provides Coach Pitino a bird's-eye view of the practice facility below. We had anticipated a marquee office and it certainly was marquee.

As a senior guard at UMass in 1974, Coach Pitino averaged 28 points per game. As a freshman, he teamed with "Dr. J" Julius Erving.

Still not knowing if we were going to have the opportunity to ask our short set of questions, we asked Coach Pitino if he had time and he graciously invited us to have a seat in front of his desk and fire away.

We did our best to be succinct, professional and to the point, but we must've looked like 5-year-old kids on their first day of school. We were nervous by just checking in, but with no time to do final preparations and get our emotions in line, we were that much more on edge.

As I asked the first of our five questions, I thought to myself "Wow, you're staring down Rick Pitino, this is crazy! Whatever you do, don't look away and let him think that you're not giving him your full attention."

It was intimidating at first, however, Coach Pitino was extremely friendly and very eloquent. We could tell immediately why he is in such demand to speak at a variety of events.

As we wrapped up our questions and began to head for the door, we asked Coach Pitino to pose for a picture with us so we could get people to believe that we really had met with him. The situation was so unbelievable that in the picture you will notice that I am not smiling. Had I done so, I probably would've completely lost it. The fact that we had come up with the idea just days earlier and now were with a future Hall of Famer was beyond our wildest dreams.

Outside, we raced to the car and began the celebration. Not only for the fact that the interview had gone exceedingly well, but that a coach the caliber of Rick Pitino was now on board. From there, we began to believe that our crazy notion might become a full-fledged reality.

Coach Pitino began his ascent to the top as a graduate assistant at the University of Hawaii in 1974-75. He spent the next season as an assistant coach.

In front of the closed blinds in Coach Pitino's office.

Rick Pitino Profile

BORN:

September 18, 1952

HOMETOWN:

New York, New York

HIGH SCHOOL:

Dominic - Oyster Bay, Long Island

COLLEGE:

University of Massachusetts - 1974

MAJOR:

Bachelor's: Political Science

When he took the reigns at Boston University in 1978, Coach Pitino was the youngest Division I head coach in the country at the time at just 25 years old.

Rick Pitino Year-by-Year

Year	School	W-L (Pct.)	Postseason
1978-79	Boston Univ.	17-9 (.654)	----
1979-80	Boston Univ.	21-9 (.700)	NIT
1980-81	Boston Univ.	13-14 (.481)	----
1981-82	Boston Univ.	19-9 (.679)	----
1982-83	Boston Univ.	21-10 (.677)	NCAA (0-1)
1985-86	Providence	17-14 (.548)	NIT
1986-87	Providence	25-9 (.735)	NCAA Final Four
1989-90	Kentucky	14-14 (.500)	----
1990-91	Kentucky	22-6 (.786)	----
1991-92	Kentucky	29-7 (.806)	NCAA Elite Eight
1992-93	Kentucky	30-4 (.882)	NCAA Final Four
1993-94	Kentucky	27-7 (.794)	NCAA Second Round
1994-95	Kentucky	28-5 (.848)	NCAA Elite Eight
1995-96	Kentucky	34-2 (.944)	NCAA Champions
1996-97	Kentucky	35-5 (.875)	NCAA Final Four
2001-02	Louisville	19-13 (.594)	NIT
2002-03	Louisville	25-7 (.781)	NCAA Second Round
2003-04	Louisville	20-10 (.667)	NCAA First Round
2004-05	Louisville	33-5 (.868)	NCAA Final Four
2005-06	Louisville	21-13 (.618)	NIT
2006-07	Louisville	24-10 (.706)	NCAA Second Round
21 Seasons		**494-182 (.731)**	

Coach Pitino was an assistant coach with the NY Knicks from 1983-85, the head coach from 1987-89 and head coach of the Boston Celtics from 1997-01.

Interview with Rick Pitino

What has been your most rewarding season as a coach?

Pitino: As I look back, Providence College in '87 was the most mediocre team, in terms of physical talent, that I've ever coached and I probably marvel in what those young men accomplished most in all the years that I've coached.

But it was a bittersweet time for me because at the beginning of that run, I lost my son to crib death. So I never really enjoyed the emotional experience of going to that Final Four until years later looking back on it. But I marvel at that team the most, and the '97 team (Kentucky) that went back to the championship game and lost to Arizona. We lost most of our starters the year before with the championship team, and that team (in '97) was very young and went back, so I marvel at that team.

And then probably the Final Four team that was here (Louisville) wasn't as talented as some of my other Final Four teams.

I guess four of them, my New York Knicks team, the second year was very rewarding. It's tough to pinpoint a season.

Looking through your coaching stops, in the second season that you've led a team, you've done phenomenal. What's the key behind that?

Pitino: Generally, the reason that a team is floundering is in two areas: a lack of talent and secondly a lack of discipline. So it takes a year to bring in talent or to enhance the talent and to create discipline.

Discipline is generally so new the first year, the system is so new, that in the second year everything takes effect. The discipline comes to the top, the talent gets better, the players improve but in the first year, everybody struggles with something.

When a player graduates or leaves early for any number of reasons, what would you hope they take away from their time with you?

Pitino: I think that it is developing a work ethic second to none. Today, I think you are successful because of your work ethic. Everything else is important, such as networking with people. I think high integrity and all the things that your parents have taught you somewhere along the line are important.

But if you don't have a strong work ethic, I don't think you can be

Pitino is the only coach in NCAA history to lead three different schools to the Final Four - Providence College ('87), UK ('93, 96, 97), U of L ('05).

successful today, and I think that is why a lot of teams and a lot of people miss out, because they don't start with that common denominator.

If you have two recruits that are of equal ability, what differentiates them for you?

Pitino: It is something that is very difficult to judge today because our evaluation period is very limited, our time is very limited in visiting with people. Everybody is on their best behavior when you meet them so you never really get to know them.

I recruited a young man last year who ended up transferring, and I thought, based on what people told me and everything else, that he was a gym rat. Which was just the opposite, he was not a gym rat.

If I could have someone with incredible passion for what they do, that would be the difference maker, if they have unbelievable passion. Because then you know that they are going to succeed. The only ones that haven't succeeded while I've been in coaching have been the ones that have not had a great passion for what they were doing.

Syracuse coach Jim Boeheim hired Coach Pitino as an assistant on his wedding day to wife Joanne (Minardi) - April 3, 1976 in Manhattan.

Skip Prosser
June 25, 2006

We had the entire story from our June 2006 visit and interview with Coach Prosser written and ready to go, however, upon his untimely death on July 26, 2007, we felt that it was appropriate to rewrite the chapter.

Coach Prosser was the second individual that agreed to meet with us, and he went so far as to ask us when a good time for us might be. Agreeing to see us on the Wake Forest campus on Sunday, June 25, despite an overnight basketball camp in progress, we spent nearly an hour with the late Demon Deacons' leader. It felt like forever - but in a good way - especially since we had asked for just 15 minutes of his day.

It was our first experience with an Atlantic Coast Conference (ACC) coach and it was very different from what we expected. He was genuine, easy to talk with and down to earth. He didn't try to get us out of the way so he could get on with things, in fact, he asked several times if we had any additional questions.

Instead of continuing to focus on the surrounding details of our trip, we'd like to tell you more about Coach Prosser's life - where he came from, how he got started and his life as a coach and teacher to young men from across the country and the world.

Born on November 3, 1950, in Pittsburgh, Pennsylvania, George Edward "Skip" Prosser was a standout athlete at Carnegie High School in both football and basketball. From there, he enlisted at the United States Merchant Marine Academy in Kings Point, New York. Playing three years of basketball as a guard and one year of rugby while in college, Prosser graduated in 1972 with a degree in Nautical Science.

His coaching career began shortly thereafter at the Linsly Institute in Wheeling, West Virginia, where he spent four seasons as the freshman coach before being promoted to junior varsity coach for one additional year prior to taking the reigns as the head coach. His varsity record totaled 33-9 over two years at Linsly, where he also taught history.

In 1979, he accepted the head coaching job at Central Catholic High

Coach Prosser led Wake Forest to its first No. 1 ranking in the national polls in school history in 2004-05.

School where he coached for six years, amassing a record of 104-48 and claiming the 1982 West Virginia AA State Championship with a mark of 25-2. At CCHS, the Maroon Knights advanced to five regional championships under the tutelage of Prosser.

At the age of 34, in 1985, Prosser acquired his first collegiate coaching job as an assistant at Xavier University in Cincinnati, Ohio. Serving for eight seasons under then head coach Pete Gillen, Prosser helped the Musketeers to an overall record of 180-67, along with seven NCAA Tournament appearances and a Sweet Sixteen berth in 1990.

Prosser's first head coaching job at the Division I level came at Loyola College in Baltimore, Maryland, in 1993. Taking over a squad that had won just two games the previous season, Prosser led the Greyhounds to the biggest turnaround in the NCAA in 1994, finishing the year with a mark of 17-13 and earning a spot in the NCAA Tournament.

Following one season in Maryland, he returned to Xavier, this time as the head coach. In seven seasons at the helm from 1994-2001, XU tallied a record of 148-65, and made the move from the Midwestern Collegiate Conference (MCC) to the Atlantic 10 for the 1995-96 campaign.

Named the head coach at Wake Forest on April 24, 2001, Prosser led the Demon Deacons for six seasons until his death. During the period, WFU went 126-68 and made it to four NCAA Tournaments and one NIT. From 2002-2005, Wake Forest averaged nearly 24 wins per season and produced current NBA stars Josh Howard and Chris Paul. In 2003, Prosser was named ACC Coach of the Year.

He is survived by his wife Nancy and sons, Scott and Mark.

PROSSER IS THE ONLY COACH TO LEAD THREE DIFFERENT SCHOOLS TO THE NCAA TOURNAMENT IN HIS FIRST SEASON AT EACH INSTITUTION.

A conference room in the basketball offices area with a large mural present on the wall.

Skip Prosser Profile

LIFE:

November 3, 1950 - July 26, 2007

HOMETOWN:

Pittsburgh, Pennsylvania

HIGH SCHOOL:

Carnegie (Pa.)

COLLEGE:

United States Merchant Marine Academy - 1972

West Virginia University - 1980

MAJOR:

Bachelor's: Nautical Science

Master's: Secondary Education

Shortly after being informed of Coach Prosser's death, ESPN's Dick Vitale wrote: "Prosser was as good a guy as it gets."

Skip Prosser Year-by-Year

Year	School	W-L (Pct.)	Postseason
1993-94	Loyola (Md.)	17-13 (.567)	NCAA First Round
1994-95	Xavier	23-5 (.821)	NCAA First Round
1995-96	Xavier	13-15 (.464)	----
1996-97	Xavier	23-6 (.793)	NCAA Second Round
1997-98	Xavier	22-8 (.733)	NCAA First Round
1998-99	Xavier	25-11 (.694)	NIT
1999-00	Xavier	21-12 (.639)	NIT
2000-01	Xavier	21-8 (.724)	NCAA First Round
2001-02	Wake Forest	21-13 (.618)	NCAA Second Round
2002-03	Wake Forest	25-6 (.806)	NCAA Second Round
2003-04	Wake Forest	21-10 (.677)	NCAA Sweet Sixteen
2004-05	Wake Forest	27-6 (.818)	NCAA Second Round
2005-06	Wake Forest	17-17 (.500)	NIT
2006-07	Wake Forest	15-16 (.484)	----
14 Seasons		**291-146 (.666)**	

Chris Paul was the fourth pick in 2005 while Josh Howard was the 29th selection in 2003. Both were first team All-Americans under Coach Prosser at Wake.

John Beilein
August 7, 2006 & June 13, 2007

We had the pleasure of meeting with Coach Beilein twice - once while he was the head coach at West Virginia, the other after he took over the reigns at the University of Michigan.

The first occasion occurred on August 7, 2006, in Morgantown, West Virginia, inside the WVU Coliseum. A 280-mile trek from home, we entered Coach Beilein's office just before 10 a.m. having left home before the crack of dawn.

After offering us something to drink, he poured himself a cup of coffee and inquired as to what our project was all about. It was fun conversing with him, in large part because of the enthusiasm and genuine interest he showed toward our initiative.

Coach Beilein tends to look perturbed in pictures, which I felt comfortable enough to mention to him, but he really came across as a hard-working, roll up the sleeves, blue-collar kind of guy.

Following a really enjoyable 25-minute session, we exited his office and thought we were headed to the car. Instead of a final handshake, he offered to personally show us around the arena. As we descended the steps to the playing level, we were able to speak casually with Coach Beilein, a nice contrast to the sit-down interview format.

As we stood at center court, he told us about senior night in 2006, which featured names such as Gansey, Pittsnoggle, Herbert and his own son, Patrick. Coach Beilein described the volume level as 14,000 Mountaineer fans went crazy in honor of the heralded group which propelled WVU to a Sweet Sixteen and an Elite Eight appearance in back-to-back seasons.

After more than an hour, we walked back upstairs to the basketball offices where Coach Beilein signed autographs and took pictures with us before extending us that final handshake, sending us on our way up the road to Pittsburgh where we were scheduled to meet Panthers' head coach Jamie Dixon.

Ten months later, upon Coach Beilein's hiring at Michigan on April 3,

Coach Beilein is the only active leader to record a 20-win season at the junior college, NAIA, Division II and Division I levels.

2007, we immediately went to work on an encore with the veteran coach and father of four. On the morning of June 13, 2007, we met with him again in his new office and had another memorable visit.

On his coffee table was a large board with the layout of the floor inside U of M's Crisler Arena. Strong on detail, Coach Beilein had small circular wooden chips, each with a number representing 1-5 (1 being for the point guard, 2 the shooting guard, 3 the small forward, 4 the power forward and 5 the center).

Used in order to walk through practice sessions with his coaching staff, and also for one-on-one use with players, Coach Beilein views it as a great tool for those that are more visual in learning. He can devise certain situations and then show exactly where each position should move on the floor. It was really interesting to watch as he recreated the play that helped his 2007 West Virginia team advance to the NIT championship game several months earlier.

Whether in Morgantown or Ann Arbor, Coach Beilein was great to us and we think that Wolverine fans are really going to like having him as their head coach.

Coach Beilein has never been an assistant coach. He started at Newfane Central High School in Newfane, N.Y. as the head coach in the late '70s.

With Coach Beilein in Morgantown while still the head coach of the Mountaineers.

John Beilein Profile

BORN:

February 5, 1953

HOMETOWN:

Burt, New York

HIGH SCHOOL:

DeSales Catholic - Lockport, New York

COLLEGE:

Wheeling Jesuit - 1975

Niagara - 1981

MAJOR:

Bachelor's: History

Master's: Education

Coach Beilein played four seasons at Wheeling Jesuit - formerly known as Wheeling College - from 1971-75 and was team captain as a junior.

John Beilein Year-by-Year (Division I only)

Year	School	W-L (Pct.)	Postseason
1992-93	Canisius	10-18 (.357)	----
1993-94	Canisius	22-7 (.759)	NIT
1994-95	Canisius	21-14 (.600)	NIT
1995-96	Canisius	19-11 (.633)	NCAA First Round
1996-97	Canisius	17-12 (.586)	----
1997-98	Richmond	23-8 (.742)	NCAA Second Round
1998-99	Richmond	15-12 (.556)	----
1999-00	Richmond	18-12 (.600)	----
2000-01	Richmond	22-7 (.759)	NIT
2001-02	Richmond	22-14 (.611)	NIT
2002-03	West Virginia	14-15 (.483)	----
2003-04	West Virginia	17-14 (.548)	NIT
2004-05	West Virginia	24-11 (.686)	NCAA Elite Eight
2005-06	West Virginia	22-11 (.667)	NCAA Sweet Sixteen
2006-07	West Virginia	27-9 (.750)	NIT
2007-08	Michigan		
15 Seasons		**293-175 (.626)**	

On April 3, 2007, Beilein became the 16th coach in U of M history just five days after winning the NIT in New York City with the WVU Mountaineers.

Interview with John Beilein

What do you hope players take away from their time with you?

Beilein: I hope that not only do they take away with them a great basketball experience, but all the little things that go with developing as a person.

Hopefully, they are going to get a degree, but sometimes a degree is misleading - does the degree always equate to an education? A lot of times somebody gets a degree, but are they really better off in life? But that is one of the biggest things we want them to do, get a degree as well as an education with life skills.

How do you change culture when you come to a new program and get things going in the right direction?

Beilein: I know one thing, you don't come in and start kicking down doors to change cultures. There has to be some compromise made and when you go in you say, "Okay, this is what the culture is like, boy you do a lot of things really well here at Michigan, we have been very fortunate at West Virginia to do some things well, let's combine our philosophies and we should be even better if we do that."

That is the general philosophy I have used whenever I have gone into a new place. I don't know it all, but you tell me about what has worked here and let's put all of our minds together.

Where do you personally try to improve as a coach?

Beilein: I think different and more effective ways to communicate. I heard Mike Krzyzewski say this at a clinic one time, "It is not important what I know, it is important what I can get the players to know." I try to hire my staff based on their ability to communicate.

I don't see us changing a great deal in how we play, it would be more specific to what players we have...not, "Now I'm at Michigan, so we have to play differently." That's not going to happen, but maybe I'm going to inherit a different style of player. Just because our 4-man last year shot 400 three-pointers doesn't mean that our 4-man this year should shoot 400 three-pointers. No, we will tweak it to what we have.

I think that I want to communicate to our players so that they can be the best that they can be at this level. It is an area where you must always

In 2004-05, Coach Beilein guided West Virginia to the Elite Eight, their deepest tourney run since 1959 when Jerry West led WVU to the title game.

strive to improve, otherwise you get stagnant if your communication goes down.

Who were the most influential people in and out of basketball throughout your journey?

Beilein: You know there are so many people I steal ideas from, or just share ideas; it is tough to single anyone out. Tom and Joe Niland, my two uncles, one was the coach at Canisius and the other the coach at Lemoyne. Those two guys were head coaches, Division I and Division II, and they mentored me in how to coach basketball.

You know who my biggest influence is? Every player that I have ever had influences how I coach, to realize that they are all so different. I think my family has influenced how I coach knowing that my four children are very different. If you have four children from the same mother and same father so different, then you learn that your team is very different. You have to treat your team fairly, but not always the same, because they are different.

You don't come from the traditional background. What are some of the factors of success that have led you here to Michigan, having started at Erie Community College?

Beilein: The trial and error, the mistakes, and the sleepless nights, because you as a coach learn the hard way. I didn't have Bobby Knight, Dean Smith, or Jim Boeheim telling me, "This is the way you should do it if you want to win this game." You sort of lose it, and you say, "What was I thinking with two minutes to go?" Those are the big factors that have really helped me grow as a coach, trial and error.

I think we have a tough time as coaches finding out what we are doing right. It is not as hard to find out what you are doing wrong. If you have a lot of wins then you have a lot of losses. You are going to lose five to 15 games a year. If you are a really good coach you are going to lose five to 15 every year.

I just really learn from losses, and after 32 years...you learn a lot. The old quote from Dean Smith was, "If you treat every game as a life and death situation, you are going to be dead a lot."

Jerry West's silhouette is the NBA logo. In 14 seasons with the Los Angeles Lakers, West averaged 27 points per game and was a 12-time All-Star.

How was it coaching your son, Patrick, at West Virginia on such a big stage?

Beilein: I had only coached him on a Little League team when he was seven or eight, and I was a part-time coach because I had taken another job and was out of town a lot. So this was the first time I was a full-time coach with Patrick.

It is the best and worst of times when you are coaching because I think when you are coaching him and you win and he is part of it, that is a great, great feeling. When you lose and he is part of it, it is a tough feeling because you might take it a bit more personally, that your son didn't play well.

There was one thing that I caught before it was too late. I realized that after games, everyone else's parents went out to eat and he would go with other player's parents. I would usually just get a pizza to go and eat in the peace and quiet, so we finally started going out. It was a little distracting because we were at a table and people would want to come up and talk about the game, but I realized that I still wanted and needed to do it for my son.

It was very different at times, for example, I never take my eyes off a foul shooter in a big game, when a guy has to make a one-and-one, up three with five seconds to go. But my son was in those situations a lot because he was a good foul shooter and I would never look when he was shooting foul shots. He was the only guy I wouldn't look at, instead I would look back at my wife or if it was a road game I would look away.

He was the one who handled it the best, because he played with a lot of passion for his father, but he also played for his teammates. It was one of those rare situations where he got along with everybody on the team, and that does not always happen when there is a coach's son.

Patrick Beilein, Coach Beilein's eldest son, was a standout player in the Richmond, Virginia area and was going to play at UR until his dad got the WVU job.

NCAA Tournament History

1939-1950 -- District playoffs were staged with eight winners emerging for a single-elmination, eight-team tournament with the championship held in Evanston, Illinois. Oregon won the first "Big Dance" over Ohio State, 46-33. The tournament has always been a single-elmination format and remains so to this day. However, for a number of years, third place and regional runner-up games were conducted.

1951-1952 -- Expanded from eight to 16 teams with 10 squads receiving automatic bids. Coach Adolph Rupp and the Kentucky Wildcats emerged victorious, beating the Kansas State Wildcats, 68-58, in Minneapolis, Minnesota.

1953 -- Increased to 22 teams and awarded byes to six teams. Overall, the tournament witnessed play from 12 eastern teams and 10 western squads. Indiana took the title, 69-68, over Kansas. From '53 through 1974, the amount of teams involved varied between 22-25.

1975-1978 -- Expanded to 32 participants. For the first time, teams other than conference victors could be selected. However, no more than two teams per conference could gain entry. The first year in this format marked Coach John Wooden's final season as a head coach. His UCLA team won its tenth title under the "Wizard of Westwood", defeating Kentucky, 92-85.

1979 -- Ballooned to 40 teams. The top six in each region received byes while seeds 7-10 played in the first round. Earvin "Magic" Johnson and the Michigan State Spartans defeated Larry Bird and the Indiana State Sycamores, 75-64. The game remains the highest rated in the televised history of college basketball.

1980-1984 -- Expanded to 48 teams featuring 24 automatic bids and 24 "at-large" berths. The top 16 teams received a bye.

1985-Present -- Increased to 64 teams and is the tournament that we know today, featuring four regions, with 16 teams a piece. In 2000, a "play-in" game was added which matches two teams vying for the right to earn a 16-seed.

In 1966, Texas Western, now known as UTEP, won the National Championship over Kentucky, the first team ever to feature five black starting players.

Jamie Dixon

August 7, 2006

Ninety-minutes after our first interview of the day with Coach Beilein, we parked in a residential section near downtown Pittsburgh. Dave, who has a bladder the size of a thimble, had to find a bathroom before we could find the arena and Coach Dixon. We entered what we thought was a University of Pittsburgh maintained building and were told that the men's restroom was located in the basement.

Unfortunately, the unassuming building was not a university-run establishment, but that of a day care facility. The path to the restroom was barricaded by dozens of young children looking at us and wondering what business we had there. Immediately, we decided to try someplace else before inciting a riot as nap-time seemed imminent.

Not exactly sure where we were, although we knew we were close, we called Pitt SID Greg Hotchkiss and he guided us to the corner of Terrace Street and Sutherland Drive, home to the Petersen Events Center and Pittsburgh Panthers' basketball.

Where we were instructed to park was a bit tricky. I have been driving a manual transmission for longer than I've had a driver's license, but the only spot available was a narrow space between two very nice cars, located on a severe incline. With no room for error, Dave got out and helped us to avoid an unneeded fender-bender.

Entering through the loading dock, we eventually found Mr. Hotchkiss' office. Over the next hour, as we were early for our meeting with Coach Dixon, Greg guided us through the locker rooms, the attached recreation center, the McCarl Hall of Champions and the courtside suites unique to the 12,508-seat venue. The $119-million gem, which opened in 2002, is truly a gorgeous facility all the way around.

Our tour ended when we arrived at the men's basketball offices and were escorted into Coach Dixon's office overlooking the arena. During games the student section, known as the "Oakland Zoo", packs in hundreds upon hundreds of frenzied fans as they occupy a large percentage of the lower deck.

As a player at Texas Christian University, Coach Dixon appeared in 109 games and scored 885 points, an average of 8.1 ppg. for his career.

Coach Dixon offered us seats across from his desk and told us to fire away. The Hollywood, California native spent time talking about his days as a child actor in Southern California, to his assistant years at the University of Hawaii, to the transition from assistant to head coach when Ben Howland departed to accept the head coaching vacancy at UCLA following the 2003 season.

In his first year as the head man, Coach Dixon and the Panthers established a new school record with 31 wins while advancing to the NCAA Tournament's Sweet Sixteen.

Despite being in the midst of camp, his casual attire and attitude was indicative of the way the interview went. He was relaxed and possibly using the time as a break from the hectic atmosphere on the court outside and below his office.

Showing us out through the sliding glass doors overlooking the arena, Mr. Hotchkiss then provided us with several Pitt t-shirts and led us back toward our car, passing through the Beano Cook Media Room on the way out.

Somehow, we forgot to take the camera in with us and thus you will notice that we had to have a photo provided. He is the only coach that we met throughout the process that we didn't get to pose with us.

Coach Dixon was selected by the Washington Bullets, now the Wizards, in the 1987 NBA Draft and played in the CBA and overseas.

photo courtesy of Pitt sports information

Jamie Dixon Profile

BORN:

November 10, 1965

HOMETOWN:

North Hollywood, California

HIGH SCHOOL:

Notre Dame - Sherman Oaks, California

COLLEGE:

Texas Christian University - 1987

UC-Santa Barbara - 1992

MAJOR:

Bachelor's: Finance

Master's: Economics

Dixon's playing career ended in Holland when he collided with an opposing player and nearly died after rupturing his pancreas.

Jamie Dixon Year-by-Year

Year	School	W-L (Pct.)	Postseason
2003-04	Pittsburgh	31-5 (.861)	NCAA Sweet Sixteen
2004-05	Pittsburgh	20-9 (.690)	NCAA First Round
2005-06	Pittsburgh	25-8 (.758)	NCAA Second Round
2006-07	Pittsburgh	29-8 (.784)	NCAA Sweet Sixteen
4 Seasons		**105-30 (.778)**	

With 105 wins in his first four seasons, Coach Dixon ranks behind only N.C. State's Everett Case for the most wins in a coach's initial four years.

Interview with Jamie Dixon

You were at Hawaii as an assistant for several years. How do you recruit in Hawaii?

Dixon: You just have to find your niche, just like anywhere you have to find what works. We went through a period of adjustment where we always would recruit junior college kids because they had been away from home once already, so they have had that experience of dealing with being away from home.

You do not have a lot of homegrown guys in Hawaii, so I started getting us into foreign recruiting. If a guy from Europe is going to travel 4,000 miles to the states, what is 3,000 more to get out to the islands? The key was to determine whether or not you were being tricked, because you did not want a guy who just wanted to take a trip to Hawaii that was not really serious about the school. You did not want to waste a trip for a recruit that might not be as serious, so that was a concern we had.

Obviously getting them out there wasn't always easy, but once they were out there the basketball atmosphere was good, and the crowds were good. They built a brand new facility while I was there, all the games are on television locally, and there are no professional teams to compete with, all good selling points. It is a great place, I loved it there, and I met my wife there.

What was it like growing up in the Hollywood area?

Dixon: My parents are from New York so we always spent time going back and forth between New York and Hollywood. So even as a kid in New York I always got asked what it was like in Hollywood. I always knew it was interesting to other people, but it really was not that much different.

I guess it is more about the people who raise you, and my parents are from New York so they had their way of life and their way of doing things. You did have kids doing the child actor thing. Everybody did it, I mean the same kids that I was playing Little League with were the same kids that were doing the interviews for commercials, so I got used to the Hollywood atmosphere. But all in all, sports were a big part of growing up, and that is what I was interested in, so it was good.

Dixon was an assistant coach at the University of Hawaii on two separate occasions. First from 1992-94 and then for the 1998-99 season.

When Coach Howland accepted the job at UCLA, how was the transition from assistant coach to head coach at Pittsburgh?

Dixon: That is something that is talked about all the time, and my thing was to not make it that big of a deal, because that is how I felt.

I didn't want to change and become a different person when I became the head coach. These kids knew me too well through recruiting or coaching, so I was not going to change who I was to somebody I wasn't. That is the last thing I want to do is to trick players, so I always try to stay the same, be the same person.

The media makes it bigger than it is, the transition that is, but even as a player, as an assistant coach and as a graduate assistant, I have been preparing for this day all my life.

What type of players are you looking to recruit and what are the selling points of Pittsburgh?

Dixon: I think a lot of things. You have to be willing to adapt, be willing to change when times and location changes. You cannot rely on one certain place; we have not had a lot of players in the Pittsburgh area so we have had to go to other areas to recruit.

But we have to keep grinding away, and we try to stay within Big East cities, so the kids can play in front of their family and friends. Initially, we felt Ohio would be a great place to recruit, but that is Big Ten country. However, the Big East has expanded with Cincinnati, DePaul, and Marquette and is getting a little more Midwest flavor. You have to figure out who can play, and it is even harder to figure out who you can get.

What do you hope players take away from their time with you?

Dixon: I want our guys to play after college, and play at the highest level in the NBA because that is good for us and for them, so good all around. Also, going overseas to Europe and understanding the value in that and understanding that is a good first job for a 21-22-year-old.

I want them to have a good experience. A lot of the guys want to get into coaching, which means to me that they had a good experience in college playing basketball, and that the players come together as a team and understand diversity.

Born in North Hollywood, California, Coach Dixon remains a card carrying member of the Screen Actor's Guild.

Bruce Weber

August 16, 2006

The good ol' alarm clock went off at 4:30 a.m. and six hours later, Dave and I exited I-74 and began weaving through Champaign. Passing through much of the modest town of approximately 75,000 we eventually sailed past the University of Illinois campus and were forced to turn around at an outlying farmstead, silo included.

Soon we found Assembly Hall as well as the Illini practice facility, the $5.5 million Richard T. Ubben Basketball Complex, right across the street. Making the parking lot our dressing room, we soon checked in with the secretary in the Ubben building. We were told that Coach Weber had stepped out but would be back shortly.

Outside the entry door to the basketball office is the practice floor, located on the bottom level. On top, you can traverse two sides of the court and get a quick history lesson of Illinois basketball, as there are numerous pictures and banners representing legendary teams and players.

We milled around for about 10 minutes admiring the facility before we decided to wait in the office area for Coach Weber to arrive. Shortly thereafter he walked in, introduced himself and escorted us back to his office.

Instead of sitting behind his desk, Coach Weber pulled over a third chair from the other side of the office and sat down next to us in front of his desk. His office was full of mementos and as you might expect, a number of them were from the 2004-05 season in which the Illini reached the NCAA title game and were a handful of possessions away from the first undefeated season since Indiana in 1976.

Energetic and extremely open to our questions, we talked with Coach Weber for almost 45 minutes. He spoke fondly of his time with Coach Gene Keady at Purdue and also his first head coaching stop at Southern Illinois, just down the road in Carbondale. He also chronicled for us the difficulty in acquiring his first collegiate coaching job for the Hilltoppers of Western Kentucky, also with Coach Keady, as a grad assistant in 1979.

Through four seasons at the helm of the Illini, Coach Weber has won 112 games, an average of 28 victories per season.

Coach Weber drove down to Bowling Green, Kentucky, to interview for the open position at WKU. However, at the time, Coach Keady was in Colorado Springs working with USA Basketball. Upon his return, Coach Keady made a number of calls to the Milwaukee area to learn about Coach Weber. After checking the facts, Coach Keady didn't make Coach Weber drive back to Kentucky to offer him the job, he extended it to him right over the phone.

Following the interview, we walked across the street to Assembly Hall and trekked nearly all the way around the structure in order to find an open door. Little did we know that once we got in, we would have just as much trouble getting out.

Assembly Hall opened on March 4, 1963, and when you see it on television, filled by 16,618 Orange Krush fanatics, it is an intimidating venue. But on the day that we visited, the place was nearly empty with the exception of a handful of workers who were setting up for a concert. The basketball floor was not in place and when vacated, the arena is fairly dark and drab. However, on game day the vibrant fans really make it come to life, offering the Illini a huge home-court advantage.

We were in business attire and wanted to exit the arena closest to the car because as the thermometer on that day read more than 90 degrees. However, every set of doors that we approached was equipped with small, wooden padlock-like blocks which prevented them from opening. After about a dozen failed attempts, we finally got out, nearly back to the spot where we had entered.

By winning 37 games in 2004-05, Illinois tied the NCAA Division I record for most wins in a single season (Duke '86, '99), (UNLV '87).

In the background on the wall of Coach Weber's office hang pictures of Assembly Hall filled to capacity.

Bruce Weber Profile

BORN:

October 19, 1956

HOMETOWN:

Milwaukee, Wisconsin

HIGH SCHOOL:

Milwaukee Marshall

COLLEGE:

University of Wisconsin-Milwaukee - 1978

Western Kentucky - 1981

MAJOR:

Bachelor's: Education

Master's: Education Administration and Physical Education

Also in 2004-05, the Illni rattled off 29 wins to start the season and finished the regular season at No. 1 in the Associated Press poll.

Bruce Weber Year-by-Year

Year	School	W-L (Pct.)	Postseason
1998-99	Southern Ill.	15-12 (.556)	----
1999-00	Southern Ill.	20-13 (.606)	NIT
2000-01	Southern Ill.	16-14 (.533)	----
2001-02	Southern Ill.	28-8 (.778)	NCAA Sweet Sixteen
2002-03	Southern Ill.	24-7 (.774)	NCAA First Round
2003-04	Illinois	26-7 (.788)	NCAA Sweet Sixteen
2004-05	Illinois	37-2 (.949)	NCAA Runner-Up
2005-06	Illinois	26-7 (.788)	NCAA Second Round
2006-07	Illinois	23-12 (.657)	NCAA First Round
9 Seasons		**215-82 (.724)**	

In his final two seasons at Southern Illinois, Coach Weber led the Salukis to a record of 52-15 and back-to-back Missouri Valley Conference titles.

Interview with Bruce Weber

What type of things do you hope that your players take away from their experience with you, or what life lessons would you hope to teach them?

Weber: You hope it is more than just basketball, and I take pride in helping them learn about life. For some kids it is as basic as getting a checkbook and a driver's license.

It is more than basketball - it is life lessons, it is networking, and dealing with people, and so many other things that can help them become successful. My goal is for my players to have a chance to be successful in life, and if it is not basketball, can they graduate and get a decent job? Can they hold that job? Can they communicate? I understand that everyone cannot be a success story, but most of the guys that have stayed have gotten degrees. So you are proud of that and it gives them a chance to be successful in life.

In 2004-05 you won 37 games, how did you deal with the pressure during that time?

Weber: Well, the biggest thing we had to deal with that year was the constant media attention and fan attention - it was a rock concert and it kept building as we kept winning. It seemed like the kids played relaxed, maybe it was because one of their goals was the Final Four and not going undefeated.

The other part, with the autographs and the people, it just got out of hand. At the hotels we had special security, we had guards on the floors, and we had to come through the kitchen elevators. The internet guys hired people, the balls were going for $500-600 because we had a chance to go undefeated.

We had calls where people would say, "We have room service for you, what room are you in?" Well, it was autograph guys trying to get to our room, and they stalked us! It was fun at the beginning but it just wore off. The guys were so good at signing autographs and that is something I would talk about all the time with networking and shaking hands. You never know if that kid for who you signed an autograph has a dad who could be a millionaire and hire you someday. We would talk about that stuff all the time.

With his first collegiate coaching job in 1979-80 as a graduate assistant to Coach Gene Keady at Western Kentucky, Coach Weber earned just $2,000.

What about dealing with pressure since 2005?

Weber: Well, the whole thing is that you win 30-some games, the most in the history of the game, and are a couple possessions away from being 39-0, but coaches know and people around basketball know that it has happened only three times, ever.

In 2006 we won 26 games, and it was the fourth most in (Illinois) history and yet it was a letdown. We were a tenth of a second away from tying for the Big Ten again, and then a crazy game with Washington in the Sweet Sixteen, we get a call or a bounce, who knows what happens. I think the true fans appreciate it, but the jump on the bandwagon type people don't understand.

But I will tell you this; our kids expect to win, because they don't know any different. So I think that helps your program because some programs don't know how to win, or kids don't understand it, but our kids expect it and understand the work ethic that it takes.

Who have been your influences in and out of basketball?

Weber: My father and mom, they sacrificed a lot with five kids, all of us coaches. Neither of them had a college education; my dad came over on a boat from Austria, and they both sacrificed for us to have a chance, and gave us a work ethic and an opportunity.

Then Coach Keady, there is no doubt that he gave me a chance as a grad assistant. I was with him a long time and had unbelievable experiences at Purdue, USA Basketball, just so many things. Basketball has allowed me to travel the world. Coach Keady gave me opportunities, and taught me about basketball, winning basketball. He taught me a lot about life, life lessons.

All my years there I saw so much and dealt with so many things through him that when I became a head coach an incident would occur and history just repeats itself, just a different person, a different place. Those people have been the most influential for me, and they have given me a shot in the business.

You talk about "no job is beneath you", where did this mentality originate?

Weber: Well, I think that comes a little bit with being an assistant for so long. I wasn't a star player, but starred as a grad assistant. I think it is

Coach Weber spent 19 years as an assistant coach under Coach Keady - one season at Western Kentucky and 18 at Purdue.

just the team, and if I do it then everyone feels good about it. Whether it is taking the bags off the planes, passing out sandwiches, helping grab the laundry, I don't care what it is.

They'll get mad at me here saying, "You're the coach at Illinois!" Does that mean that I have to walk around in some fancy thing and not do anything and be a jerk? One of the worries people had when I got a head coaching job was, "Can he delegate?" I think that I have done pretty well, I still want to know what is going on, I want to help, and I want to be a part of it, but I have learned to delegate.

At Purdue, I was there for so long I did camps, I did tickets, and I did travel. I got tutors and actually I was the tutor for a long time. I did study tables - we didn't have academic advisors when I started and that is how I approached it. I love running camps - people think I am nuts and say "Why are you here for camps?" Well, it is our camp, and I think I should do camp. I like working with kids, and if it influences somebody then I'm doing my job.

What are the biggest differences coaching at the mid-major and Big Ten levels?

Weber: At this level you become more of an ambassador for the university. If you have success like Coach Keady, his name is synonymous with Purdue, Coach Knight at Indiana, Coach Wooden at UCLA, and Coach Smith at North Carolina.

At Southern Illinois, people in town knew me, but you didn't have that national recognition because you weren't on TV all the time. I think coaching-wise you get a better athlete, maybe a little better prepared kid, but our kids at Southern worked just as hard, if not harder, so that is maybe why we won because we approached it no differently. You eat the $16 steak instead of the $30 steak, little things like that.

I had to do laundry. On Christmas day the equipment guy didn't work, so I brought home the laundry and my wife and I did practice jerseys. We had to fundraise at Southern just to survive, which here at Illinois I have to do some things for the "I Fund" and that, but it wasn't my responsibility to get money so we could eat on the road. But it was fun, there are great memories.

WHILE AT PURDUE, COACH WEBER HELPED THE BOILERMAKERS TO SIX BIG TEN CHAMPIONSHIPS AND 14 NCAA TOURNAMENT APPEARANCES.

After being an assistant for so long, what was the process like of becoming the head coach at Illinois?

Weber: I was at Purdue for a long time, five years at Southern wasn't that long, but I turned down a job every year there. That was the ironic thing, I couldn't get a job for 18 years, but every year (at SIU) I had offers, and some years more than one.

But I wasn't going to leave. I promised the people there I wouldn't leave unless it was a huge step up and a great job, hopefully a Big Ten job, so it all worked out.

What do you do to get away from hoops?

Weber: I walk every morning and also try to walk every night. I try to help around the house and get my kids to school. We walk the dogs, my wife and I, and that is our time to catch up and find out what is going on in each other's life. Late night, I watch ESPN and that is my time.

Coach Weber played point guard at Milwaukee Marshall High School and also played catcher for the baseball team.

Bo Ryan
August 16, 2006

Before leaving Illinois, we decided to take one more shot at Wisconsin and Bo Ryan since we were relatively close to Madison. Previously, it didn't look like it was going to work because the Badgers were getting set to depart on a week-long trip to Italy the following morning.

Will Ryan, Coach Ryan's eldest son and director of basketball operations at Wisconsin at the time, answered our call and offered to give us a personal tour of Wisconsin's arena, the Kohl Center. A half hour into the 250-mile drive from Champaign to Madison, the phone rang and the caller identification said that it was Will.

Before answering, we suspected that things had changed and that we could no longer view the facilities at UW. We were way off. Instead of canceling, Will informed us that he had talked to his father about our project and that Coach Ryan wondered if we'd like to come to his home to conduct an interview, but only if we had time.

If we had time? We did, but even if we didn't, we would've made time, no question about it. On television, Coach Ryan appears to be someone who could inflict damage both physically and verbally, but how bad could he be? How often are you going to find a high profile coach, who is leaving the country the next morning, invite two guys whom he has never met over to his home?

Following some slow-going rush hour traffic, we parked directly in front of the Kohl Center and inserted several coins into the meter. On most college campuses the parking enforcement people are sticklers and we didn't want to chance it at Wisconsin either.

Meeting Will at the door, we followed him upstairs to the basketball offices and were introduced to his younger brother Matt, who also works full-time with the program and manager Mike Gard.

From there we spent better than an hour touring the 17,190-seat arena, named for Sen. Herb Kohl after he donated $25 million to the efforts. Built in 1998, the ice was open for hockey so we never saw the basketball court, but we saw everything else, including the men's basketball locker

Coach Ryan spent eight seasons in the late '70s and early '80s as an assistant coach at Wisconsin before taking the UW-Platteville job in 1984.

room which combines a lounge, dressing area and shower facilities.

Finishing the tour, we grabbed the unticketed car and met Will and Matt around the block and wove through the busy streets of Madison. About 25 minutes after leaving the Kohl Center, we pulled into Coach Ryan's driveway and were led inside by the brothers.

Coach Ryan met us in the foyer near the kitchen and immediately made us feel welcome. We followed him into his office, which is lined with mementos from his time at Wisconsin-Platteville, where in 15 years Coach Ryan won four Division III national championships. In the last five years of his tenure there, he compiled an unbelievable record of 138-8 and finished with back-to-back national championships and undefeated campaigns.

While Coach Ryan finished up a few things in his office for their pending trip to Italy, Will and Matt gave us a tour of the house. Highlights included a theater room, an indoor pool with a heated floor as well as a workout facility and several large decks overlooking the wooded landscape. The house is big, don't get us wrong, but it isn't gaudy by any means. Despite its size, the Ryan home was inviting and mirrored the character of their family.

Soon thereafter, Coach Ryan showed us out to the deck located off the living room and for more than an hour we talked hoops as darkness approached. When the mosquitoes started to bite, we went back inside the house and were promptly asked by his wife Kelly to join them for dinner before heading for home.

Somewhat stunned and taken aback, we were reluctant as we didn't want to overextend our welcome. However, they insisted, and for the next hour we sat eating and casually conversed with four members of the Ryan family.

By 10 p.m., after spending nearly four hours at Coach Ryan's residence, he posed for a picture with us in front of former Wisconsin All-American and current Dallas Maverick Devin Harris' signed and framed Badger jersey.

As our visit wrapped up, we received directions from Kelly and talked as we exited through the front door. In the driveway, I told Coach Ryan that I had accidentally scratched his car on the way into the house. Instantly he looked like he was going to be sick. Of course I was kidding. It just goes to show how relaxed and comfortable we became around Coach Ryan and his family after only a few hours of time.

On February 19, 2007, the Badgers acquired the ranking of No. 1 in the nation for the first time in school history.

Inside Coach Ryan's home in Madison with former UW All-American Devin Harris' signed jersey is in the background.

Bo Ryan Profile

BORN:

December 20, 1947

HOMETOWN:

Chester, Pennsylvania

HIGH SCHOOL:

Chester

COLLEGE:

Wilkes (Pa.) College - 1969

MAJOR:

Bachelor's: Business Administration

A Badger from 2001-04, Devin Harris was selected fifth overall in the 2004 NBA Draft by Dallas. In 2006, the Mavs reached the NBA Finals.

Bo Ryan Year-by-Year (Division I only)

Year	School	W-L (Pct.)	Postseason
2001-02	Wisconsin	19-13 (.594)	NCAA Second Round
2002-03	Wisconsin	24-8 (.750)	NCAA Sweet Sixteen
2003-04	Wisconsin	25-7 (.781)	NCAA Second Round
2004-05	Wisconsin	25-9 (.735)	NCAA Elite Eight
2005-06	Wisconsin	19-12 (.613)	NCAA First Round
2006-07	Wisconsin	30-6 (.833)	NCAA Second Round
6 Seasons		**142-55 (.721)**	

The head coach at NAIA/ NCAA Division III Wisconsin-Platteville for 15 seasons, Coach Ryan won 353 games, an average of 23.5 per year.

Interview with Bo Ryan

After a player leaves your program, for whatever reason, what do you hope they take away from their time with you?

Ryan: My expression has always been "I want you guys to be good neighbors." Well what does it take to be a good neighbor? You are considerate of other people, you help in the community, but first you take care of your own house with your family, and then take care of your neighbors. So I want my players to be people who take with them a sense of their work is not done.

Just because you played, or you have your degree, there are certain things you need to do. Hopefully they give back to the school, but more importantly they give back to the community. I hope they take that with them.

Your road to Division I head coach has been unconventional, was Division I your ultimate goal?

Ryan: It would be what people would want to hear. But do you know that when I coached in high school, I thought that was the only place that existed in the country? When I was at Sun Valley High School, which you guys have never heard of, I thought the world started and ended there. When I coached in junior high, during the season there was absolutely nothing else that entered my mind.

If you think for one second that I didn't think about, at times, coming back to where I was an assistant, back to where I thought we were just a little short, we didn't win any championships when I was here during those eight years. You can't tell me when I was watching Badger games when I was at Platteville and Milwaukee that something doesn't say, "Wouldn't it be nice to be at *the* university in the state?" Yeah…but I never let it get in the way of the kids that I was coaching at the time.

At Platteville, you don't have scholarships and you still rack up national title after national title and 30 wins, what is the secret? How did you do it so consistently?

Ryan: That first group, I had a couple of assistants that for no money beat the bushes and got a recruiting class of a combination of Wisconsin and Chicago kids, young men. A lot of people say that state schools, they

Under Coach Ryan, the Pioneers reached postseason play 13 out of 15 years and won four National Championships ('91, '95, '98, '99).

are not as expensive and it is easier to get students, but that is not true at Platteville.

But here is what happened, that first group in '91, then off of that group, guys just became believers. Any kid who was going to be in engineering in northern Illinois or Wisconsin, that wanted to play basketball came to Platteville. We beat the bushes and found some raw, hungry kids, and mixed them in with some very steady, good shooters.

Don't play Division III schools in "Horse". The reason they didn't get scholarships, most of those guys, is because they weren't athletic enough. Well, in Division III, you got a lot of guys that can shoot. We ended up with a good combination, and we had a system, we had the swing offense. People can say whatever they want about it, but you change parts, inside, outside, bigs can step out, smalls can go in the post, a lot of basket cuts off of screens, back screens, we got a system going.

With teams, I have never compared one to another. When you get something going, the upperclassmen as they move from underclassmen to upperclassmen, they pass it along to the new guys. We think we have got that going a little bit here at Wisconsin.

The main thing was to get a group that can establish the tradition and never let it die. You are going to have some dips in there, but try to make sure that the players who won, the younger ones, always remember and pass it along to the next group that is coming in and try to keep it going. I don't think it was anything that I did as a coach. I think it was more what we got the players to do who had the experience to be able to pass that on to the younger players the next year.

In and out of coaching who has been influential to you?

Ryan: My dad of course, because your parents are your first teachers. He is a legend back in the Philly area. Everybody knows him because he has coached so many kids. In his youth he was asked to leave two high schools. He was a juvenile delinquent who ended up going into the Navy after lying about his age. He fought in WWII in the South Pacific and has a Bronze Star.

When he came out (of the Navy), he would come home from work, grab a couple pieces of bread and cheese and go either to the baseball diamond, the football field, or the basketball court. He coached those three sports and coached thousands of kids. So that is what I grew up in.

IN 2007, THE PLAYING SURFACE INSIDE WILLIAMS FIELDHOUSE AT UW-PLATTEVILLE WAS RENAMED "BO RYAN COURT".

How is it working and coaching along with your sons?

Ryan: I never bring it home, they don't know if we had a bad practice, a good practice, or anything in between. I am very fortunate. You cannot coach - like a lot of professions - you cannot take on a passionate occupation that is very time consuming and draws a lot of energy from you and still be able to do the family thing unless you have a great family. They are the ones who help me be able to do what I do.

How do you take a step away from basketball?

Ryan: I hated golf, but now I like it because it gets me outside, it is my contact with nature because I don't get to fish, and I don't get to do the other things very much. So golf is an escape, but it also takes a lot of time. I play it, but I refuse to take lessons until I retire.

I'll do the golf outings for charities, for the university, some social golf, but I refuse to take lessons and be obsessed with it. So that is kind of an escape, things with the family, and reading, of course.

If you could put a criticism on yourself when you self-examine, where do you think you could be better as a coach?

Ryan: Oh patience, without a doubt. I think everything should be done right now, don't you? You need to be a better ball handler right now, don't turn the ball over. I have been working on my patience since 1972 when I got out of the Army and got my teaching degree and decided to coach in junior high school.

But I think I'm getting better at it. Just being a little more patient at times, but I would rather have that then be the kind of coach that isn't too excited about the game, or passionate about it. I think it is the passion that I have for the game that makes me impatient as a coach.

How does it feel to be one of the nation's elite coaches?

Ryan: It is our job to be facilitators for these young men to have the best experience they can. Winning is more enjoyable than losing, period. So I think athletes have a better experience, if they have some success.

People can say what they want to about losing, or not making the tournament, but there will never be a replacement for the experience that these guys get as student-athletes… whether you come in first or last. So what I look at is way past the numbers. I want these guys to have the

In his final five seasons at UW-Platteville from 1995-1999, Coach Ryan compiled a record of 138-8 (.945) including three DIII National Championships.

best experience they can, and it isn't always going to be fun. It is going to be a lot of work and everything else, but I want the learning experience that they have to be as enjoyable as it can be.

Therefore, success, I think is a part of that equation, and needless to say with coaches that is how we are always judged. If we want to help these young men, keep your jobs, don't take shortcuts, because if you do, they might. They feed off of us, and we feed off of them. I feed off of their energy, it keeps me young.

It still has to be about the experience that is our main function in life, because somebody did it for me. We spend more time in our lifetime with coaches than we do with teachers and a lot of the friends that we have. So we better take what we do very, very seriously, because we have the opportunity to impact the lives of young people.

Everyday I go to the Kohl Center and I know what I've got in front of me - a chance to influence and to help young people. Hopefully, they will then help other young people. I view it as a coach that we are in our timeline, we are influencing another timeline that is going to influence another timeline, and to me that is a pretty good profession to be in.

His son, Will, now an assistant coach at North Dakota State, played on two National Championship teams at Platteville - 1997-98 and 1998-99.

Thad Matta
August 23, 2006

There are two stories from our time in Columbus that we think you'll find interesting. The first was one-on-one with Ohio State's Thad Matta on August 23, and the other came on January 26 and 27 when ESPN's "GameDay" rolled into the land of the Buckeyes. We'll start with our experience at "GameDay".

On Friday afternoon, the day before Michigan State came into the Schottenstein Center to play Ohio State, we found ourselves sitting in the ESPN truck, listening to the production meeting with Rece Davis, Jay Bilas, Hubert Davis, Digger Phelps, producer Lee Fitting and others from ESPN such as Barry Sacks, Nick Loucks and Howie Schwab. Months earlier when first meeting Jay, he invited us to see the show first-hand.

The following morning, we walked out to the court with Schwabie and watched the show from behind the cameras. After it concluded, we went out for lunch and came back to watch some of the action from the afternoon games in the truck.

During the late afternoon hours, Dick Vitale arrived from Sarasota, Florida, and we soon went with Howie to Dicky V's pregame suite inside the "Schott". For several hours, the pair prepped for the game, going over notes, statistics and individual player reports. Listening intently, we occasionally got to chime in with our thoughts. If we know any one team in particular, it is the Ohio State Buckeyes.

As game time approached we headed upstairs to the "GameDay" suite where they broadcast the pregame and halftime segments. We took the batteries out of our cell phones for the live show and then grabbed a seat as Greg Oden, the 2007 No. 1 overall NBA Draft selection won the tip for OSU.

By halftime, the Buckeyes had a commanding 43-23 lead and it looked like we might be going on national television. Before the game, we talked with ESPN reporter Erin Andrews who had been informed of our story by Doris Burke, who you'll hear more about later.

Erin told us if the game was a blowout, our chances were very good

Coach Matta played three seasons at Butler University, lettering two, after transferring from Southern Illinois University in Carbondale, Illinois.

that we would go on the air. However, they had to first stay with the game and the surrounding storylines.

With a 20-point margin at the break, we went to courtside to get ready. Right out of the chute, Michigan State began to whittle into the lead and thus we never got on TV. The Spartans ended up taking Ohio State down to the wire, missing a three-point field goal at the final buzzer to preserve a 66-64 victory for the Buckeyes.

Our trip to meet with Coach Matta was relatively short as we left home at 7 a.m. and returned before 2 p.m. - lunch included.

Setting up the interview was also unusual. Working with Bowling Green men's basketball throughout my time in college, one of our assistants, LaMonta Stone, used to be an Ohio State coach. He is friends with the Buckeyes' associate head coach John Groce, whom he called on our behalf to arrange a time with Coach Matta in his office.

Scheduled for 10 a.m. on August 23, we entered the enormous Schottenstein Center, talked our way through a series of offices and finally located the men's basketball area. Coach Matta was in a staff meeting across the hall, but soon emerged and headed right for us with his right hand extended.

Talk about a normal guy, he was as down to earth as it gets. He told us about how much he enjoys mowing his lawn, and that since he can no longer do it consistently because of time constraints, how much he gets on the lawn service people to cut straight lines.

Being respectful of time, like with every other coach, he was surprised that we really did want just a few minutes. He even gave us a perplexed look and said, "You're kidding?" when we said that we were finished.

As a result, he offered up several stories from his coaching tenure at Xavier and about the Lawrence North duo, Greg Oden, the No. 1 overall NBA Draft pick in 2007 to the Portland Trailblazers and the No. 4 overall pick to the Memphis Grizzlies, Mike Conley.

Before leaving, Coach Matta gave each of us a signed photo and asked us to excuse his shoes in the picture as it was unexpectedly taken soon after he had finished mowing his yard!

In 1990-91, Coach Matta began his coaching career as a graduate assistant under Tates Locke at Indiana State.

Inside Coach Matta's office in the Schottenstein Center.

Thad Matta Profile

BORN:

July 11, 1967

HOMETOWN:

Hoopeston, Illinois

HIGH SCHOOL:

Hoopeston-East Lynn

COLLEGE:

Butler University - 1990

MAJOR:

Bachelor's: Education

Matta worked as an assistant at Butler and Miami (Oh) on two separate occasions each - Butler (1991-94 & 1997-00) and Miami (Oh) (1994-95 & 1996-97).

Thad Matta Year-by-Year

Year	School	W-L (Pct.)	Postseason
2000-01	Butler	24-8 (.750)	NCAA Second Round
2001-02	Xavier	26-6 (.813)	NCAA Second Round
2002-03	Xavier	26-6 (.813)	NCAA Second Round
2003-04	Xavier	26-11 (.703)	NCAA Elite Eight
2004-05	Ohio State	20-12 (.625)	----
2005-06	Ohio State	26-6 (.813)	NCAA Second Round
2006-07	Ohio State	35-4 (.897)	NCAA Runner-Up
7 Seasons		**183-53 (.775)**	

A 40-year-old in 2007, Coach Matta has already spent time coaching in the Big Ten, Missouri Valley, Horizon, Southern, Atlantic-10 and the MAC.

Interview with Thad Matta

What do you hope your players take from their time with you?

Matta: First and foremost, I hope that they feel we treated them the right way, and we made them better people, better players and prepared them for life.

I always tell kids that my job as a coach will not be judged until the kids I coached are 40 years old. Hopefully they have a beautiful family, a beautiful home and their 401k plans are in check. At that point, I will know that we helped that kid, and I think the biggest thing we strive for is to treat them right, make them better and help them achieve the goals that they have when they get here.

Who have been the biggest influences on you, in and out of hoops?

Matta: Obviously my mom and dad. My dad was a coach and an athletic director, and all I ever wanted in life was to be him. I wanted to coach in a little town in Illinois because we had such a great life.

It is funny how we look and see how times change. We ate breakfast every morning together and dinner together every night. Every night my dad was home and tucking me in bed. Now, I can go three weeks without seeing my family. So the values I was taught by my mom and dad, I could never put a price on those.

Then Barry Collier, who is now the AD at Butler. What he did for me as a coach, I played for him for a year, he brought me back as a coach, and in essence he got me the Butler job when he left for Nebraska. So I am forever indebted to him.

Then a guy named Tates Locke, he gave me my first start at Indiana State right out of college. Tates was a guy who gave Bobby Knight his first start at Army, Bobby Knight was his assistant. Another influence is a guy like Herb Sendek at Miami (Ohio), who taught me the value of recruiting.

All of those guys come together and form who I try to be, not who I am, but who I try to be. I have been very fortunate who I've had along my path. And then Charlie Coles (head coach at Miami), who is like my second father because we were assistants together, and then I worked for him when he became the head coach. So I think it has been a conglomeration of people who have shaped and molded me as a coach.

Coach Matta led Xavier to 26 wins in each of his three seasons and helped Xavier reach the Elite Eight in 2004, the best finish in school history.

My best friend, my wife, is the greatest coach's wife, and understands my position and supports me when I am gone with raising the family. She is someone I turn to and I envy the position she is in.

You've been at three different levels - mid-major, elite mid-major and now high major at Ohio State. How do you go about recruiting and the process as a whole?

Matta: When you are at a place like Butler, I think I have always been this way… I was trying to pull the No. 1 recruiting class at Butler. I had more holes in my back from being shot down and kids saying no.

In all places that I have been, I have always viewed it as a special place and people don't believe this, but every job that I have had is the greatest job that I have ever had, and opportunities, God-willing, have presented themselves for me.

But at a place like Butler, you are a little more centrally located in your recruiting, and you are not looking at the elite of the elite players.

At Xavier, it was odd because we were in the A-10 so we could recruit the East Coast because we played so many games out there. Once again, we did most of our recruiting centrally, and even at Xavier we battled everyone for kids.

When we got here (Ohio State) we were at rock bottom of college basketball, and we took a calculated risk of spending more time with the juniors, with five scholarships to give to the senior class because we got the job so late. Our thing was to build this program the right way, and once again with Ohio State the thing I found was the power and magnitude of this university. I had no idea. I didn't know nationwide what this university was made of with the alumni base.

What were the biggest factors for you becoming a head coach by the age of 33?

Matta: (pause)... Luck! Number one, first and foremost. A lot of guys have asked me, younger coaches, "How did you do it, get to Ohio State? And I tell them I am the luckiest guy in the world." I thank God everyday for the things he has done, by pointing me in the right direction and putting me in the right places.

It is funny because the night Barry Collier called me to come back to Butler, I was at Miami (OH), I hung up the phone and said to my wife, "I

THE BUCKEYES ADVANCED TO THEIR NINTH FINAL FOUR, AND FIRST SINCE 1968, FINISHING AS THE NATIONAL RUNNER-UP TO FLORIDA IN 2006-07.

have no interest in going back to Butler." And my wife and I both went to Butler. So I called Charlie (Coles) and told him what was up with Butler and I will never forget what he said.

He said, "Oh, you better take a look at that." And I said, "Yeah, but we have Szczerbiak, Davis, Newble, Estes, and Friarson... we are going to go to the Sweet Sixteen!" And he said, "Thad, Barry Collier is going to leave and you are going to be the next head coach at Butler!"

Honestly, I really owe Charlie for pointing me in the right direction. But it is something with the goals and the things I wanted to do, you have to have a plan to be striving for something everyday when you wake up.

When I went back to Butler as an assistant, I thought, "I will be the next Bill Guthridge (UNC). I love Butler and I'll stay here forever and be Barry's right-hand man." I have never been one of those guys who make calls for a job, things have just fallen my way… knock on wood.

What's your relationship with Coach Tressel and football?

Matta: Coach Tressel has been great, he has been a tremendous asset to me personally and to our program. It is shocking how he has gone out of his way to help us, from recruiting - I help them with recruiting too - to pointing me in the right direction about Ohio State and Columbus.

It is funny during Big Ten play, every morning at 6 a.m. I get a text message from him on game day, and it became a standing joke, but also a ritual in pregame. The kids would say, "What did Coach Tressel have to say today?" And I would pull out the text and read it to them. But Jim is a unique guy, I have never met someone with more passion for Ohio State or the state of Ohio and for us to walk kids in on a football Saturday is just amazing.

What is in the future for Buckeye basketball?

Matta: We are trying to sustain the contender status and do it the right way. From academics, to the social, to who we bring in and how we carry ourselves. To me that is what the program is all about, and that is what I want, is a program.

For me personally, I love Columbus, I love Ohio State, and I love the challenge of waking up every morning, and trying to build this program. People think that we have arrived, and in my mind we aren't even close.

Ohio State won the NCAA title in 1960 and reached the championship game in 1961 and 1962, led by stars Jerry Lucas and John Havlicek.

Commonly Asked Questions...

Throughout the entire process, we've gotten a number of questions, and most times, a number of them are the same. As a result, we decided to include the answers to a few of our most asked. However, e-mail us if you'd like to know more:

dh@destinationbasketball.com

What was your favorite experience?

Andrew: I really enjoyed going to Los Angeles. Being from Ohio and the country, I had never been out there. And while I don't have intentions of moving to LA, it was fun to see the differences from around here. One place advertised a "deal" on a haircut for a guy - $85!

Dave: Mine was without a doubt our weekend in NYC. We got to sit courtside in Madison Square Garden, we appeared on national television and I also got to see my college buddy Stephen Trafton perform on Broadway's "Les Miserables".

Who was your favorite coach?

This is pretty tough to answer, for obvious reasons. The fact that each coach in the project agreed to meet with us was incredible. However, for me, there were three guys whose personalities really jumped at me - Thad Matta, John Beilein and Rick Barnes. I felt similar in attitude to each of them.

Dave particularly enjoyed speaking to John Chaney because of his passion for education, and also Coach Self because of his Down-to-Earth persona, especially with the pressure that he is under at Kansas.

Who was the toughest coach to meet with?

The guys on Tobacco Road were probably the hardest to acquire, especially all at the same time. A number of coaches required months of phone calls and e-mails, but never did we have to turn a "no" into a "yes".

On February 13, 1954, Frank Selvy scored 100 points for Furman. He is the only player in Division I history to score 100 points in a single game.

Tom Izzo
September 2, 2006

We walked up to the Magic Johnson statue entitled "Always a Champion", located just outside the Breslin Center at approximately 9:10 a.m. and met with SID Matt Larson shortly thereafter. He led us into the lobby of the Michigan State men's basketball offices, situated inside the Alfred Berkowitz Basketball Complex, which is attached to the Breslin Center. Immediately the 2000 national championship trophy came into view, proudly on display within a glass case, tinted Spartan green by back lighting.

Waiting for Coach Izzo to arrive, Mr. Larson provided us with a full tour of the facilities in the Berkowitz Complex, including the wall of pictures that leads you down a hallway to Coach Izzo's office, representing all of the former Spartans to have played, or who are currently competing in the NBA.

At 9:45 we were led into Coach Izzo's beautiful corner office which features glass windows from floor-to-ceiling on two sides, allowing you to look out over the MSU campus. The sun-drenched view on that morning was of anxious fans arriving to tailgate for the football season-opener against the Vandals of Idaho which kicked off at noon.

Coach Izzo offered us seats in a little meeting area of his office and began inquiring about the project as a whole. For nearly half an hour he gave a great interview. He was just as intense in talking as he appears on the sidelines during a game. Whenever he wanted to emphasize a point, his hands would propel forward and his feet would tap the floor to match the syllables in his words.

Following the interview, as Coach Izzo prepared to depart and join the Spartan faithful for his traditional Saturday morning tailgating tour, we were escorted through the practice facility by Mr. Larson and got a chance to see inside the Michigan State locker room. There the jerseys of former Spartan greats line the halls. Names like Mateen Cleaves, Jason Richardson, Zach Randolph and Earvin "Magic" Johnson, who led MSU to their first of two national championships in 1979 over Larry Bird and

In 1972-73, Coach Izzo walked on to the basketball team at Northern Michigan and finished as a Division II All-American in 1976-77.

the Indiana State Sycamores.

Magic went on to become a 12-time NBA All-Star, averaging 19.5 points, 7.2 rebounds and 11.2 assists for the Los Angeles Lakers. Still to this day, that championship holds the record for the highest-rated NCAA basketball game in television history.

As we made our way out to the car, we spent another half hour or so tailgating with the Spartan football fanatics who were already partying it up. The season didn't go nearly as well as hoped on the football side of things, but on that day the Spartans won, 27-17.

Coach Izzo was inducted to the Northern Michigan University Hall of Fame in October 1990.

Near the entrance to Coach Izzo's corner office which overlooks the Michigan State campus.

Tom Izzo Profile

BORN:

January 30, 1955

HOMETOWN:

Iron Mountain, Michigan

HIGH SCHOOL:

Iron Mountain

COLLEGE:

Northern Michigan University - 1977

MAJOR:

Bachelor's: Physical Education

Coach Izzo gave his son, Steven, the middle name "Mateen" after point guard Mateen Cleaves who starred at MSU in the late '90s.

Tom Izzo Year-by-Year

Year	School	W-L (Pct.)	Postseason
1995-96	Michigan St.	16-16 (.500)	NIT
1996-97	Michigan St.	17-12 (.586)	NIT
1997-98	Michigan St.	22-8 (.733)	NCAA Sweet Sixteen
1998-99	Michigan St.	33-5 (.868)	NCAA Final Four
1999-00	Michigan St.	32-7 (.821)	NCAA Champions
2000-01	Michigan St.	28-5 (.848)	NCAA Final Four
2001-02	Michigan St.	19-12 (.613)	NCAA First Round
2002-03	Michigan St.	22-13 (.629)	NCAA Elite Eight
2003-04	Michigan St.	18-12 (.600)	NCAA First Round
2004-05	Michigan St.	26-7 (.788)	NCAA Final Four
2005-06	Michigan St.	22-12 (.647)	NCAA First Round
2006-07	Michigan St.	23-12 (.657)	NCAA Second Round
12 Seasons		**278-121 (.697)**	

Every four-year player under Coach Izzo while the head coach at Michigan State has been to a Final Four - 1999, 2000, 2001 and 2005.

Interview With Tom Izzo

You went from a walk-on to an All-American playing basketball at Northern Michigan, can you talk about that process and evolution?

Izzo: It happens a lot easier in Division II than Division I. You know, I was fortunate enough to be in the right place at the right time, which for the most part is how my life has gone.

Even here, I was fortunate enough to be an assistant when Jud (Heathcote) got too old, so I got the job. In college, I had an opportunity, I went there, I did walk-on, one kid became ineligible, and some kids quit and left the team. We started out with 25 kids on the team because there was freshman ball back then, and by the end of the year we were down to 15, and I just kind of worked my way in.

Did I get better? Of course I got better, and I was fortunate to be around some of the guys that I hung with. Steve Mariucci was my best friend and roommate so we worked out together all summer. We just got better, but at the same time I had a very unique opportunity.

Who have been your influences in and out of basketball?

Izzo: I think where I grew up, everybody's father was an influence in their life. Mine was too because he was just a blue-collar guy who owned his own business, so I started working for him when I was 12. He worked a lot of hours and worked hard and that is where I got that mindset at a young age.

I was very fortunate too that I had a lot of great teachers and coaches throughout my childhood. When you come from a small community, you are kind of raised by the whole community, not just your parents. Your neighbors, the chief of police is on the backside, the principal is on the left, and someone else is on the right, so you kind of grow up differently than you do in bigger cities. I had a lot of great influences.

And when I came here Jud Heathcote was a regular guy who worked his tail off to get here. So where I was from, I came to the right place, to work for a guy who came from North Dakota and lived in Montana, the great outdoors of America, just like I did.

Jud had great knowledge, but also great insight on how to deal with certain situations. Being here 12 years I was a sponge, so no question, other than my father, Jud was the greatest influence on my life.

When Edgar Wilson left MSU in October 1983, Izzo was promoted to full-time assistant after having spent two months as a part-time assistant.

What do you hope kids take away from their time with you?

Izzo: Number one, that they understand that they will only get out of something what they put into it. Life is not fair, so do not be looking for that to be the case.

Also, there are different types of people in this world. There are some that tell you what you want to hear, and others tell you what you need to hear. I hope that I tell them the need to hear things.

I would say that you don't just always outwork people. You can go into anything that you do, for the rest of your life, and you can say, "No one is going to work harder than I am." It does not make you the best, you still have to have knowledge of the subject matter, but at least you will have a fighting man's chance.

I try to teach my guys that physical and mental toughness is the key to success in life, that you are going to have to work for anything that is good. I hope they take those things with them.

Assessing yourself as a coach, what aspects do you try to work on to get better?

Izzo: I think the hardest thing for me to deal with as a coach is never forgetting where you came from and I don't mean just the Upper Peninsula, but people try to people pick you apart when you have success and failure.

If I have one thing that I struggle with as a coach, it is the tough love thing, finding out when am I doing someone a favor and when am I hurting them. In other words, I wear my emotions on my sleeve, and I get in my players' face, but I also spend an enormous amount of time with them. I feel it gives me a license, in my mind, that they know why I am on them. But other people do not always know why I am pushing them.

Sometimes when the media gets on you for this or that and you don't want to have that image, you struggle with what you do. As a result, I might not push a kid as hard and I see him not end up in a Final Four, or with an NBA contract, or not graduating, or whatever our goals were together and I end up blaming myself saying, "You let that kid down."

What I am constantly trying to get better at is figuring out that I have a tough job, and that I have 12 or 13 different guys, different races, different backgrounds, but their goals are the same.

Coach Izzo left MSU in 1986 to take a position at Tulsa, only to return the same year when Mike Deane left for the head coaching job at Sienna College.

I am not sure that I want to be patient because I have a small window with my players. I have at most four years with them, and a lot of times it determines the girl they marry and the life they will live, by what you do in college and the image you portray, and that is all in that little window. I always hear about having patience, but patience is something I don't know if I want to have, I would rather have understanding. Everybody is going to move at a different speed. But the venue I am in, with how long you get to graduate, how long you get to become an NBA player, how long you get to win a national championship, how long you get to set your footprint in the sand here, that doesn't have any patience, so how can I?

What are your thoughts on the recruiting process as a whole here at Michigan State?

Izzo: Recruiting is the worst part of the job, because it has gotten to the point where there are too many people involved. There are too many people that do not have anyone's best interest in mind, and I struggle with that. I also struggle with being able to go into a kid's home and telling the kid what he wants to hear instead of what he needs to hear. I'm not a very good used car salesman, and I don't want to be a good used car salesman.

But I think I am a decent recruiter because we try to get in on kids early and spend a lot of time. I recruit more Michigan, Indiana, and Ohio for a reason. We could go more nationally, but I like having kids up here on football weekends, and if they can come up more often when they are sophomores and juniors, they get to know you better. It is just a better marriage, as I like to call it.

I think the perception is that every kid loves the game and that every kid wants to work his tail off to get better. Well, I think for the most part 90 percent of people in America want to be good people but not 90 percent of people work on being good people. The same with basketball, you have to find those guys and that is the hardest part because too many people get involved and you cannot climb into somebody's heart.

Aside from talent, what are ideal characteristics you are looking for in a recruit?

Izzo: If I can find some guys that are willing to work, obviously they

In 1997-98, Coach Izzo was named the Associated Press' National Coach of the Year after guding the Spartans to the Sweet Sixteen and a mark of 22-8.

have to have some skills, but if I find guys that work, then I have enough faith that we have a blueprint here academically, athletically and socially that will get them to the stage they want to get.

I think everybody has some system in which players set goals, but I am big on players taking ownership of the program. Even though people might think I am a dictator because I am tougher on the kids, I am about as far from that as you can get. I mean I don't think that you can have success unless everybody is on the same page, and everybody has common goals.

A lot of people talk about team, team, team. Well, I have team goals here and individual goals here because I think if you don't have individual goals then we are living in a vacuum. You are going to want to do what is best for the team but we are all selfish to a certain extent, you better be, so it is better to define your own personal goals. I have my guys write down five or six goals that they want to accomplish each year, and I make sure that at least two of them are individual goals.

So if a guy wants to be an All-American, wants to graduate with a certain grade point average, wants to win a national championship, wants to be an NBA player, then the way I look at it if he accomplishes some of his personal goals, then the better chance we have at accomplishing the team goals. That is my job, to put the two together.

But if I want just to get team goals, then I think I am missing the boat this day and age, because 90 percent of the guys I recruit think they are NBA players.

So I really do spend a lot of time talking about individual goals, and selling that I care about what is important to you, and that I have a job here so you better care what is important to me, so everyone is happy.

When you think rebounding you think Michigan State, where did your philosophy on rebounding originate from?

Izzo: If you want the truth, my rebounding philosophy started because my first team was such a poor shooting team, that we had to offensive rebound, so it started by default.

I just realized that defense is an aggressive thing and rebounding is really a toughness thing. That is where our toughness started, and that is why I started selling it. That is why for a couple of years we might have been the toughest team to ever play the game.

A year later, MSU advanced to the Final Four for the first time since 1978-79 when they won the championship with Earvin "Magic" Johnson.

Bill Self
September 23, 2006

I was talking to the mechanic at the local body shop when my phone started vibrating around noon on Friday, September 22. Momentarily, the phone beeped to let me know that I had a voice mail. The area code on the number was 785, unknown and very different from our local 419.

The message was from Kansas SID Chris Thiesen, wanting to know if we could meet with Coach Self the very next night in his luxury suite at the KU football game against South Florida.

Immediately I called Dave at Baldwin-Wallace, and asked if there was anything monumental looming that could possibly prevent us from making the 13-hour trip to Lawrence. There wasn't, so I quickly called Mr. Theisen and graciously accepted his invitation.

It was our longest trip to that point and our farthest distance west. Once we found our way on campus around 4 p.m. local time, we parked about two blocks from Phog Allen Fieldhouse and literally ran to the arena to meet Mr. Theisen who was waiting for us.

He was very accommodating and gave us a 30 minute all-access tour of "The Phog". We entered the Jayhawks' locker room and were advised not to walk on the huge Jayhawk logo embedded in the carpet in the center of the room out of respect to the tradition of Kansas basketball.

KU players are each equipped with a wooden locker that inside holds a nameplate. On that nameplate reads a list of Jayhawks that occupied the space prior to the current player.

"The Phog" itself has a classy and nostalgic feel. The history alone with names like James Naismith, Forrest "Phog" Allen, Dean Smith and Wilt Chamberlain makes the facility daunting to opponents. Not to mention the overhead banner that reads, *"Pay Heed, All Who Enter: Beware of "The Phog"*.

After the tour we made our way down the side streets of Lawrence, many of which are represented by names of states. At a local grocery store on Massachusetts Street, we were forced to buy a disposable camera as we had left our digital in Ohio. Soon we returned to spend

A native of Oklahoma, Self was a four-year letterwinner as an Oklahoma State Cowboy in Stillwater from 1982-85.

more time alone in Allen Fieldhouse, illuminated only by the afternoon sunlight streaming through the balcony windows.

With a 7:00 p.m. kickoff time approaching, we headed across the KU campus, picked up our media credentials outside of Memorial Stadium and made our way to our seats on the sixth story along with actual members of the media.

Coach Self was at his son's baseball game and his exact arrival time was unknown. We sat in anticipation and tried to calmly enjoy the game in front of us, which was difficult to say the least. When Coach Self arrived just before halftime, he walked through the back of the press box unannounced to most of the media present, and headed down the private hall to the basketball suite. As halftime began, Mr. Theisen grabbed us and told us to wait at the edge of the hallway as he tracked down Coach Self.

The Jayhawks' head coach soon greeted us with a firm handshake and a look of disbelief as Mr. Theisen informed him of our 13-hour trek from Ohio to Kansas with less than one day's notice. Amid the madness of the halftime media circus, we found an open table and sat down with Coach Self. With all of the people that wanted to shake his hand and talk to him, it made us feel even more fortunate to get to spend a few minutes of time with the head men's basketball coach at the University of Kansas.

Minutes after starting the interview, Max Falkenstien, the "Voice of the Jayhawks" for 60 seasons walked by and Coach Self introduced us to the award-winning announcer and informed him of our project.

Despite the distractions, we had an easy flowing conversation. The amount of respect that Coach Self has for the tradition of KU basketball was terrific to hear.

Since we were in barbeque country, and since we had also forgotten the ham sandwiches, we were looking forward to a good meal before making the return trip home.

After the third quarter we headed for Gates Barbeque in downtown Kansas City. It was quite possibly the best meal of our lives. We ordered the sampler and had a plethora of meat, drenched in Kansas City barbeque sauce. If you're ever in the Kansas City area, do yourself a favor and stop in for a meal at Gates.

We probably shouldn't have, but we drove the entire distance back to Oak Harbor through the night and into most of the morning. We were gone a total of 32 hours with nearly 27 behind the wheel.

In 1985-86, Coach Self was on Larry Brown's KU staff that went 35-4 and advanced to the Final Four, losing to Duke in the semifinals, 71-67.

In the pressbox during halftime of the Kansas football game.

Bill Self Profile

BORN:

December 27, 1962

HOMETOWN:

Edmond, Oklahoma

HIGH SCHOOL:

Edmond

COLLEGE:

Oklahoma State University - 1985

Oklahoma State University - 1989

MAJOR:

Bachelor's: Business

Master's: Athletic Administration

In his third and final season at Tulsa, Coach Self led the Golden Hurricane to a school-record 32 wins and advanced to the Elite Eight.

Bill Self Year-by-Year

Year	School	W-L (Pct.)	Postseason
1993-94	Oral Roberts	6-21 (.222)	----
1994-95	Oral Roberts	10-17 (.370)	----
1995-96	Oral Roberts	18-9 (.667)	----
1996-97	Oral Roberts	21-7 (.750)	NIT
1997-98	Tulsa	19-12 (.613)	----
1998-99	Tulsa	23-10 (.697)	NCAA Second Round
1999-00	Tulsa	32-5 (.865)	NCAA Elite Eight
2000-01	Illinois	27-8 (.771)	NCAA Elite Eight
2001-02	Illinois	26-9 (.743)	NCAA Sweet Sixteen
2002-03	Illinois	25-7 (.714)	NCAA Second Round
2003-04	Kansas	24-9 (.727)	NCAA Elite Eight
2004-05	Kansas	23-7 (.767)	NCAA First Round
2005-06	Kansas	25-8 (.758)	NCAA First Round
2006-07	Kansas	33-5 (.868)	NCAA Elite Eight
14 Seasons		**312-134 (.700)**	

Coach Self spent seven seasons - 1986-1993 as an assistant at Oklahoma State. During that time, the Cowboys advanced to five NCAA Tournaments.

Interview With Bill Self

What do you hope that players take away from their experience with you?

Self: What I hope they take away with them is that in life it is not about you, but it is about how you can make others better, which would then come back to you.

So many times people see it as what they can get out of it, and they don't understand that when you give, give, give you will also get so much more in return. Also, the fact that there are no free lunches in life, and unless you win the lottery, you are going to have to work. Usually hard work pays off, but it is not guaranteed. So when guys leave us and if they do lose their job, have family problems or any negative impact in their lives, they are quicker to handle that.

This job is described as your dream job, as it would be for a lot of people. Can you sum up the job as the head coach at KU?

Self: Definitely it is everything I thought it would be, maybe even better than I thought it would be, and I thought it would be great.

If I could sum up anything, the right word would be caretaker, because it is such an honor and great responsibility to be a caretaker of a program with such great names such as Naismith, Dean Smith and Chamberlain. It is an awesome responsibility to sit in that chair.

The media gives you a lot of attention for not yet making a Final Four, what would a Final Four mean to you professionally and personally?

Self: In a lot of ways, in other people's minds, by going to a Final Four or winning a national championship it will validate a career, but in coaches' eyes we don't see it that way. Coaches should be judged by whether they maximize their team, and the postseason is one way of doing that.

But it is hard to be recognized unless you do well in March, and I certainly understand that, but I do not feel I have to do anything to validate how I coach. Just because you win a game by a point, or because someone is injured, does not make you a better coach. You just have to put your players in the best position to win, and hopefully over time that will be in big games.

In 1988, "Danny (Manning) and the Miracles" defeated Oklahoma to win the National Championship with an overall record of 27-11.

What season has been your best coaching job?

Self: The team that we had at Tulsa (99-00) was a great team. Whenever you are a 4-point favorite to beat (North) Carolina to go to the Final Four and they upset you... that is a pretty satisfying season.

At Illinois, my first year was pretty good and the pieces all fit. I would say probably the best job our staff has done, in my mind, was my second year at Illinois when we were 4-5 in the league and ran the table to tie for the league (title), and at the end of the year we were playing for the Big Ten Tournament title as the 4-seed.

How is the whole process of recruiting kids in Lawrence, Kansas?

Self: The thing about it is, when people think of Kansas they think of western Kansas because of Dodge City and the Western movies, but once you get to Lawrence it is the far from that.

So whenever we can get kids to campus, if we can get them here, they will immediately think that it is better than they thought because of the stigma. Then you come to a game in Allen Fieldhouse and they realize there are not too many places like this in the whole country.

I think there are some positives even though there is a stigma, just getting them here will make a difference. On a scale of 1-10, it is about a 9.5 getting them here, I mean if you do your job recruiting them, they are going to take a serious look at you. Most kids that we go in it with will at least come for a visit.

What sets a kid apart? When recruiting what are you looking for?

Self: There are a couple of things about high school kids. If the freshmen that you recruit come into the situation thinking they that know everything, it will be a tough time. But if they come into the situation believing that they don't know, then they become sponges and very coachable. I would say it is something you don't know until they get here.

The other thing is that there are very few freshmen that can come in and be the man, the same role they left back in high school. The best freshmen are the ones that understand how to make others better and the team better, rather than cater to themselves. The kids that understand how to play and make others players better will be the best.

MANNING, THE 1988 CONSENSUS NATIONAL PLAYER OF THE YEAR, SCORED 31 POINTS IN THE TITLE GAME AND 2,951 FOR HIS CAREER, AND IS CURRENTLY A KU ASSISTANT COACH.

As a player at Oklahoma State, what lessons did you learn to prepare you for coaching?

Self: One of the things that helped me more than anything was that I was a slow-learning, average-talent guy that was able to play at a high level primarily because I tried hard.

You try so hard, and you learn to take short cuts and understand how to compensate for things. There is a myth out there that great players become great coaches because the game was so easy for them. In reality, it is hard to translate that to guys that the game doesn't come that easy to.

When I was growing up I played against stronger, more physical and more talented kids and that helped to make me become a better coach. I had to learn how to dissect situations and understand the mental part of the game.

Influences in and out of the game?

Self: The guy who helped me more than anyone without question, helped me build my foundation, who I learned the most from, and who I learned my philosophy from was my father.

He was a coach himself, and he molded me into believing a certain way, and made me understand that it is not a good or bad shot if it goes in, it is a good or bad shot when it leaves your hand. There are certain things you cannot control and you have to do everything to put yourself in the best position.

Then after him, the best coach I have ever been around is Larry Brown, and I learned more from him in those nine months than anybody, because I was still so young and didn't know anything. There was still so much to learn.

Then Leonard Hamilton had a great, great influence on me, and really taught me a lot about recruiting and handling people and generating energy and enthusiasm.

And I think Coach (Eddie) Sutton was one of the great coaches and deserves to be in the Hall of Fame. His strength was creating a family situation and not beating yourself, that you have to make other players beat you.

Wilt Chamberlain was a two-time All-American at Kansas in the mid-50s. He went on to average 30 points and 23 rebounds through 14 years in the NBA.

A Lot of Wins...

Coach	Wins	Losses	Pct.
Bob Knight	890	363	.710
Dean Smith	879	254	.776
Lute Olson	781	280	.736
Mike Krzyzewski	775	261	.748
Jim Calhoun	750	328	.696
Jim Boeheim	750	264	.734
Denny Crum	675	295	.696
John Wooden	664	162	.804
Gary Willliams	585	328	.641
Gene Keady	550	289	.656
Roy Williams	524	131	.800
John Chaney	516	253	.671
Rick Pitino	494	182	.731
Rick Barnes	418	220	.655
Kelvin Sampson	403	223	.644
Tubby Smith	387	145	.727
Bill Self	312	134	.700
Ben Howland	296	140	.649
Billy Donovan	296	123	.706
John Beilein	293	175	.626
Skip Prosser	291	146	.666
Tom Izzo	278	121	.697
Jay Wright	248	155	.615
Mike Brey	241	130	.650
Bruce Weber	215	82	.724
Mark Few	211	52	.802
Thad Matta	183	53	.775
Bo Ryan	142	55	.721
Jamie Dixon	105	30	.778
TOTALS	**13,152**	**5,374**	**.710**

Legendary Kentucky Coach Adolph Rupp, for whom the UK arena is named after, compiled a record of 876-190 (.822) over 41 seasons.

Kelvin Sampson

September 30, 2006

We were able to schedule an interview with Coach Sampson on a Saturday morning inside Assembly Hall at the end of September. Oak Harbor is approximately 300 miles from Bloomington and we departed at 5 a.m. in order to give ourselves time to get down there for our 11 a.m. appointment.

When you head down Route 37 south out of Indianapolis and are headed toward IU, you can just feel basketball. Martinsville, Indiana, is located on Route 37 about 20 miles north of the IU campus and served as the childhood home to legendary coach, John Wooden.

At Martinsville High School, he was an all-state performer and led his team, the Artesians, to a state championship in 1927 and two other finals appearances in 1926 and 1928. Following high school, he went on to play for Indiana's rival Purdue, located in West Lafayette, Indiana. Wooden became a three-time consensus All-American and helped the Boilermakers win the 1932 national championship.

To the south of Bloomington is the tiny village of French Lick, best known as the hometown of Larry Bird, who originally enrolled at Indiana University before leaving and playing at Indiana State University in Terre Haute, 77 miles west of Indianapolis. Bird went on to become the 1979 consensus National Player of the Year and led the underdog Sycamores to the 1979 national championship game where they were defeated by Magic Johnson and Michigan State.

We've been to Bloomington several times now, which is a beautiful tree-lined town, crazy about the Hoosiers, particularly Indiana basketball. Yet knowing that you're going to Assembly Hall to meet the head coach - that was sensational!

At about 10:15 we pulled into the parking lot and made sure everything was set to go with the interview before going inside at about a quarter until the top of the hour. We checked in with long-time secretary B.J. McElroy in the basketball offices, located up the twisting ramp on your left as you enter the main doors, and she called downstairs

Coach Sampson's first collegiate head coaching job was at Montana Tech, located in Butte, Montana, approximately 70 miles from Helena, the capital.

to where Coach Sampson was working out.

Assembly Hall is a relatively old building, as it opened for the 1971-72 season. But when an arena has been host to numerous national championship teams, and one of the best teams in college basketball history - the 1975-76 squad which finished undefeated - it is special. In the same way the old Boston Garden, Phog Allen Fieldhouse at Kansas or even places like Fenway Park (home of the Boston Red Sox) or "The House that Ruth Built", Yankee Stadium are special.

Downstairs we knocked on a locked door and it was answered by Coach Sampson. Just finishing up a workout, he invited us to sit down on a nearby couch and we spoke for better than a half hour on everything from his first head coaching job at Montana Tech to his decision to leave Oklahoma and take the reigns at one of the most basketball-rich schools in the country.

As we finished up what we felt was a solid interview, Coach Sampson led us back up the stairs to the main lobby where we got a picture together. We then shook hands and made our way back to the car for the return trip to Ohio as Coach Sampson ascended the ramp toward his office.

In 2007, Coach Sampson donated $50,000 in order to help the Montana Tech Orediggers renovate their 2,000-seat gymnasium.

In the lobby near the main entrance of Assembly Hall.

Kelvin Sampson Profile

BORN:

October 5, 1955

HOMETOWN:

Pembroke, North Carolina

HIGH SCHOOL:

Pembroke

COLLEGE:

UNC-Pembroke - 1978

Michigan State University - 1980

MAJOR:

Bachelor's: Health and Physical Education and Political Science

Master's: Coaching and Administration

Following the 1994-95 season, his first at Oklahoma, Coach Sampson was named Associated Press National Coach of the Year.

Kelvin Sampson Year-by-Year (Division I only)

Year	School	W-L (Pct.)	Postseason
1987-88	Wash. St.	13-16 (.448)	----
1988-89	Wash. St.	10-19 (.345)	----
1989-90	Wash. St.	7-22 (.241)	----
1990-91	Wash. St.	16-12 (.571)	----
1991-92	Wash. St.	22-11 (.667)	NIT
1992-93	Wash. St.	15-12 (.556)	----
1993-94	Wash. St.	20-11 (.645)	NCAA Second Round
1994-95	Oklahoma	23-9 (.719)	NCAA First Round
1995-96	Oklahoma	17-13 (.567)	NCAA First Round
1996-97	Oklahoma	19-11 (.633)	NCAA First Round
1997-98	Oklahoma	22-11 (.667)	NCAA First Round
1998-99	Oklahoma	22-11 (.667)	NCAA Sweet Sixteen
1999-00	Oklahoma	27-7 (.794)	NCAA Second Round
2000-01	Oklahoma	26-7 (.788)	NCAA First Round
2001-02	Oklahoma	31-5 (.861)	NCAA Final Four
2002-03	Oklahoma	27-7 (.794)	NCAA Elite Eight
2003-04	Oklahoma	20-11 (.645)	NIT
2004-05	Oklahoma	25-8 (.758)	NCAA Second Round
2005-06	Oklahoma	20-9 (.690)	NCAA First Round
2006-07	Indiana	21-11 (.656)	NCAA Second Round
20 Seasons		**403-223 (.644)**	

On March 29, 2006, Coach Sampson became the 26th leader of the Indiana Hoosiers men's basketball program.

Interview with Kelvin Sampson

What do you hope the lessons were that were taken away by the kids?

Sampson: How to overcome adversity and how to look at obstacles and adversity as an opportunity to get better rather than an obstacle not being able to be overcome.

Also, how to become a good teammate - how to share and how to give back. I mean, those are two critical things that we try to teach kids, that in life you're going to have obstacles and adversity, but that's okay. Some people look at obstacles and adversity as something that is hard and can't be overcome. And then others look at it as an opportunity to get better.

Who has been your biggest influence?

Sampson: My father. He was recently inducted into the North Carolina High School Coaches Hall of Fame, a great coach. He did more with less than anyone that I've ever seen. He was a coach at a little high school with not a lot of talent which typically finished seventh or eighth every year before he arrived, and he always finished first, second, or third. I learned how to coach a team and how to get your kids to play as a team.

And then at this level, it's Jud. Had it not been for Jud Heathcote giving me a chance, a guy that he didn't even know at Michigan State as a grad assistant when I was 22 years old, right out of college, you don't get here (Indiana).

My goal out of college was to be a high school coach and I was at Michigan State just getting a Master's Degree. I went in and asked Jud if it was okay if I do this, of course he found a way to say no twice and then I kind of had to give him an idea of how I could help. He was kind enough not to deny the help.

Overview on being the head coach at a school like Indiana?

Sampson: I'm not sure that I had any expectations, you know? I'm a coach, I love basketball. I feel a kinship with a lot of the fans because they love basketball and they look at it as something that is bigger than all of us, and I'm proud to be here. I'm honored to be here.

You'd like to look forward and say this is how it is going to turn out,

Coach Sampson worked for Michigan State legend Jud Heathcoate in 1979-80 as a grad assistant, a year after the Spartans won the NCAA championship.

but you don't know. I'm a simple person. I refuse to make anything complicated. I'm a basketball coach.

I had a great mother and father, they taught me to understand right from wrong. That doesn't mean that I haven't made mistakes, but the key to making mistakes is that you learn from them. And the thing that I like about being at Indiana is that these people love basketball and they honor it and I'm going to do my best to give them a great product.

Is there a certain aspect that you look to improve upon as a coach?

Sampson: Yeah, maybe trying to relax more. I don't think that is something that I could do when I was younger. I think there's two kinds of fear; I think there is a restricting type of fear and a positive type of fear and to me it has always sat right on my shoulder. I always felt like if I didn't outwork people and push because of my background and how I was raised and how I had to coach, we wouldn't survive.

I was at Montana Tech, it's an engineering college, where every curriculum required a minimum, a minimum, of 30 credit hours of math. And so I had to coach a certain way. Then you go to Washington State, which is arguably the toughest job in the Pac-10. It was a job that you had to work your butt off. And I've kind of had that mentality, it is the way that I've always coached.

Now, I don't want to lose my edge, but I think I have to learn to relax, be a little more patient, too. Jud used to say that you have to learn to coach with one eye open and one ear closed and that is probably something that I need to do a little better.

You have successfully recruited a lot of junior college players. Where did that philosophy originate?

Sampson: It's where I've coached. When I got to Washington State it wasn't one of those jobs where you beat people with the top high school players.

Spokane is a very rural area. It is in the state of Washington but it is almost 300 miles from Seattle. It is only about 70 miles from the University of Idaho, it is closer to Montana than it is to Seattle so it is remote. You have to win, so you have to figure out a way to compete. At Washington State, that is where I developed my philosophy with the junior college kids.

After the 1984-85 season, Coach Sampson left Montana Tech and spent three seasons as an assistant at Washington State before becoming the head coach.

Biggest draw in making the switch to Indiana and the biggest difficulty in leaving Oklahoma?

Sampson: The difficulty was tremendous. I had to give up the chance to coach my son to come here and he was the guy that kind of put it into perspective. He said, "Dad, how many coaches would turn down the opportunity to coach at Indiana? It is something that you have to do." And that came from my son, so that tells you something about him.

And then my wife, she is my best friend, someone for whom I have tremendous respect. We spent 12 years at Oklahoma but it tells you also about how special Indiana is in terms of the basketball community.

I started thinking about where I came from, how I got into coaching, how lucky I've been my whole life and how many people could do what I did had they gotten the opportunity.

I've just never really taken myself too seriously. I know where I came from, how I got into this stuff, how this whole thing works. You get good in this business when you have good assistants and a chance to coach good players.

I kept arguing against why I should go because I had my best recruiting class coming in and I felt like it was my program at Oklahoma. It was my school and my program, just like I'm sure Bob Stoops (OU football coach) feels the same way about it.

And then I kept thinking, "Well, but it is Indiana." I said, "I'm 50 years old and I've always looked at things from a best-case scenario and a worst-case scenario." And I started thinking, "What is the worst thing that could happen to me here at Indiana?" Think about it, it isn't that bad.

What happens if you never try? I started thinking about the lessons that I've taught my kids over the years. The first step on the ladder of success is usually failure. We have a lot of work to do here. You have to work at this stuff and there are no guarantees, but I was at a point where I said, "You know what, I'm going to try. And I'm going to try as hard as I can, and let's see what happens."

THE HOOSIERS HAVE WON THE NATIONAL CHAMPIONSHIP ON FIVE OCCASIONS - 1940, 1953, 1976, 1981, 1987.

A Lot of Miles...

We took 23 trips to meet with 29 coaches and two of the best on the broadcast side. On several trips, we were able to meet with more than one coach. Here is a look at the average time and distance it took to get it done.

Destination	Miles	Destination	Miles
Rick Barnes	1115	Thad Matta	240
John Beilein	460	Lute Olson	680
Jay Bilas	630	Rick Pitino	640
Jim Boeheim	538	Skip Prosser	1040
Mike Brey	360	Bo Ryan	538
Jim Calhoun	538	Kelvin Sampson	600
John Chaney	680	Bill Self	1550
Denny Crum	640	Dean Smith	328
Jamie Dixon	290	Tubby Smith	604
Billy Donovan	1996	Dick Vitale	2350
Mark Few	1330	Bruce Weber	538
Ben Howland	2129	Roy Williams	328
Tom Izzo	300	Gary Willliams	328
Gene Keady	560	John Wooden	2129
Bob Knight	2800	Jay Wright	538
Mike Krzyzewski	328		

Average Miles to and from Each Destination:

935.34

Average Hours to and from Each Destination

14 hours and 25 minutes

Total Miles Traveled:

27,125

If you were able to drive your car around the world at the equator, it would come to about 24,901 miles.

Tubby Smith
October 7, 2006

The University of Kentucky has one of the greatest basketball traditions of all-time. Producing national championships in 1948, 1949, 1951, 1958, 1978, 1996 and 1998, they rank second behind UCLA's 11 titles. When it comes to overall victories, the Wildcats are first with 1,948, ahead of second place North Carolina by 34.

Orlando "Tubby" Smith, now the head coach at the University of Minnesota, played the role of caretaker at UK for 10 seasons. Over that decade, Coach Smith stuffed his resume by averaging nearly 27 wins per season, winning five Southeastern Conference regular season crowns, five SEC tournament crowns, appearing in three Elite Eight appearances and bringing home the 1998 national championship.

Dave and I had the opportunity to sit down with Coach Smith in his office inside the historic Memorial Coliseum, the former home of the Wildcats for 24 seasons, before the start of what ended up being his final season pacing the sidelines in Lexington. The building was empty on a quiet Sunday afternoon and Coach Smith gave off a very relaxed on the surface appearance.

We may never know everything that went into Coach Smith's decision to leave one of the premier jobs in the country after the 2007 season. He had four years remaining on his contract. It is well known around college basketball that the coaching staff and players at Kentucky, along with a growing number of schools, face immense pressure from a number of angles including the media, boosters, administration and the loyal fans that support them year in and year out.

Several decades ago, the Final Four and the national championship were generally sought on a yearly basis by a small number of national powerhouse schools such as UCLA, North Carolina, Kansas, Kentucky and Indiana.

Together those five universities have combined to make 65 Final Four appearances. Today, there are less cupcakes than ever before, the "mid-majors" are closing the gap and the landscape is no longer dominated by

Coach Smith was the sixth of 17 children and grew up on a rural farm in southern Maryland.

a select few programs on a consistent basis. An ever growing number of schools are capable of going deep in the tournament, best evidenced by George Mason's Cinderella run in 2006 all the way to the Final Four.

The expectations around the country have been raised for many schools to the same level as that of a place like Kentucky. There are more national players on the scene than ever before and it is harder to win than ever before. What hasn't changed is the amount of teams in the Final Four. With a steadily increasing number of squads in contention, it causes the "big boys" to fall short of long-held expectations more often than not.

Kentucky has not been to a Final Four in nine years, the longest drought in school history, but is it all the fault of UK or should a large portion of credit go to the rest of college basketball that has elevated itself up the ladder?

Coach Smith's son, Saul, lettered four seasons for his father at Kentucky and now sits on the bench with his father at Minnesota as an assistant coach.

In Coach Smith's office at Kentucky prior to his final season in Lexington.

Tubby Smith Profile

BORN:

June 30, 1951

HOMETOWN:

Scotland, Maryland

HIGH SCHOOL:

Great Mills - Great Mills, Maryland

COLLEGE:

High Point (N.C.) - 1973

MAJOR:

Bachelor's: Health and Physical Education

A high school graduate of Great Mills (Md.), Coach Smith's first head coaching job came at his Alma Mater. He was there for four seasons and went 46-36.

Tubby Smith Year-by-Year

Year	School	W-L (Pct.)	Postseason
1991-92	Tulsa	17-13 (.567)	----
1992-93	Tulsa	15-14 (.517)	----
1993-94	Tulsa	23-8 (.742)	NCAA Sweet Sixteen
1994-95	Tulsa	24-8 (.750)	NCAA Sweet Sixteen
1995-96	Georgia	21-10 (.677)	NCAA Sweet Sixteen
1996-97	Georgia	24-9 (.727)	NCAA First Round
1997-98	Kentucky	35-4 (.897)	NCAA Champions
1998-99	Kentucky	28-9 (.757)	NCAA Elite Eight
1999-00	Kentucky	23-10 (.697)	NCAA Second Round
2000-01	Kentucky	24-10 (.706)	NCAA Sweet Sixteen
2001-02	Kentucky	22-10 (.688)	NCAA Sweet Sixteen
2002-03	Kentucky	32-4 (.889)	NCAA Elite Eight
2003-04	Kentucky	27-5 (.844)	NCAA Second Round
2004-05	Kentucky	28-6 (.824)	NCAA Elite Eight
2005-06	Kentucky	22-13 (.629)	NCAA Second Round
2006-07	Kentucky	22-12 (.647)	NCAA Second Round
2007-08	Minnesota		
16 Seasons		**387-145 (.727)**	

A 1973 graduate of High Point College in North Carolina, Coach Smith was an All-Carolina Conference player as a senior.

Interview with Tubby Smith

What do you hope players take away from their experience and time with you?

Smith: One would be the value of time, the most important resource is your time, and you have to make time for the ones you care about. Players can get caught up in so many things, it is more often than not a management of time.

I think some young people have a hard time with that, but if you organize yourself and prioritize things, then you will spend your time on quality things that are worthwhile and have meaning and purpose.

My dad use to tell me "idle time is the devil's time" so you want to be actively involved, and we try to encourage our players. That and along with all the values you learn with team sports.

Who have been your influences in and out of coaching?

Smith: There are quite a few people that have been my role models, my heroes and mentors. I have to start with my parents who raised 17 of us, and instilled the ethics and the morals that we have. As a person you've got to know right from wrong, and it starts with parenting and parenthood.

My mom and dad are people I love and care a lot about, and they taught us about hard work, sacrifice, commitment and being accountable, because on a farm you had chores that had to be done before you went in for dinner.

I tell my friends that you can't rush Mother Nature, so I think the patience you have to have to see a young man develop into a player, is the same patience you have to have on a farm watching crops, cultivating the garden, pulling weeds, nurturing the chickens, feeding the hogs, and feeding the cows. You have to do a lot around the farm, and that is how I approach coaching and teaching as well.

Then my high school coaches, I wanted to teach and coach when I was in the 8th grade going into the 9th grade, I had a guy by the name of C.C. Short, he was a math teacher who was also the junior varsity basketball coach, and he saw me playing at lunch time and asked my dad if I could try out for the team. That was going into the ninth grade. It was really the first time I had played organized basketball, and from that point on I

From 1989-1991, Coach Smith served as an assistant to Coach Rick Pitino at Kentucky before acquiring the head job at Tulsa in 1991.

said, "This is me, I'm not going back to the pigs on the farm."

NOTE: Keep in mind, this particular question dates to when Coach Smith was still the head coach at Kentucky. Following the 2006-07 season, which saw UK win 22 games and advance to the second round of the NCAA Tournament, Coach Smith decided to accept the open head coaching job at the University of Minnesota.

What are your thoughts on being the head coach at Kentucky?

Tubby: It is as good a job as there is in the country when it comes to college basketball. It has it elements you have to overcome, like most programs do. It is a little bit unique, not totally unique, but unique in that the perceptions are that we are going to win every game, or win every championship out there. But I think people appreciate how hard we work to try to be the best possible basketball program, and try to put the best product and team out on the court for each game.

It goes back to the management of time. This is a program that can consume you, there are so many other distractions if you are not careful - and I am the world's worst at saying "no" - it can consume you.

I think my main job in this position is to serve, to serve the student body, our faculty, our administration, our staff, fans, players, right on down the line, so it is a daunting task and a big responsibility, but something we take very seriously.

In 10 seasons at Kentucky, Coach Smith averaged 26.3 wins per year and reached the NCAA Tourney each season and never won less than 22 games.

Jim Calhoun
October 14, 2006

The University of Connecticut is located in Storrs, not far from the capital city of Hartford, which is not far from ESPN Studios in Bristol.

We headed for West Hartford, Connecticut, on Friday afternoon where we intended to get a hotel room for the evening, before making the short trip to the University of Connecticut in the morning.

Four hours into the drive, nearing the city of Scranton, Pennsylvania, we decided to call "The Schwab" who lives in West Hartford. A year earlier, while visiting ESPN Studios, we met Howie by pure chance, had lunch with him, and have since kept in fairly good touch.

He didn't answer, but within 10 minutes my phone was buzzing with Schwabie on the other end. Soon we found ourselves invited to the University of Hartford's version of "Midnight Madness". Knowing that we probably wouldn't be able to get there in time for the show, we set up a breakfast engagement and pressed on down I-84 through the darkness.

At 12:35 a.m., we rolled into the greater Hartford area and started looking for a hotel room that would put us in close proximity for the morning.

Seventy miles, three hours, three trips around the city and nine hotels later, we pulled into one of the nicest joints in town, priced at way more than we wanted to spend for the night. We didn't stop with hopes of getting a room, we just wanted to sleep in their safe-looking and fairly well-lit parking lot. It was 3:40 a.m.

The temperature had plummeted to 17 degrees - at least that is what the bank clock read when we passed it for the third time. Still, the frozen conditions would have been tolerable had we possessed dry blankets. Just before leaving, we took several that were in my dryer, however, they obviously hadn't gotten enough time in the hot box because they were still soaked in the middle.

We were told by the hotel front desk attendant that the hotel public bathroom would once again be operational at 7 a.m., so we would only have to suffer in the cold for a few hours. Yet by 6 a.m., after covering up

Coach Calhoun coached Reggie Lewis at Northwestern for three seasons before accepting the UConn coaching job in 1986-87 prior to Lewis' final year.

with my dress pants and a hand towel, I looked over to see Dave leaning forward, his jaw chattering with his arms tucked inside his shirt, hugging himself. What a long hour that was. I started the car a couple of times but we were both hesitant to let it run for any extended period of time for some unknown reason, probably because we knew the hotel might take issue if they saw us crashing in their parking lot.

Watching the dashboard clock like a pair of hawks, we grabbed our stuff at four minutes from the top of the hour and headed for the warmth of the hotel bathroom. Twenty-five minutes later, looking fairly presentable, we sat in the lobby, read the paper and took advantage of the free orange juice, meant of course for paying guests.

By 9 a.m., we found ourselves sitting inside "Lox, Stock and Bagel", a popular morning cafe on Main Street in downtown West Hartford. Five minutes later, in came Schwab, dressed in a Bowling Green basketball jersey that I had sent to him to wear on the show back in July.

Nearly an hour went by as we talked about the project and the forthcoming weekend, along with the coaches that we had not yet been able to acquire for an interview. As we walked out, we thanked Howie for getting up early on a Saturday to spend a little time with us and headed toward Storrs and a meeting with Jim Calhoun.

Located about 25 miles east of Hartford, we wove down a little two-lane road through dense forests, up and down rolling hills and all of a sudden arrived at the home of the basketball powerhouse that is UConn.

Once inside the 10,027-seat Gampel Pavilion at about 11 a.m., we sat with reporters for the last hour of practice and admired the high level of athleticism that has been a mainstay at UConn since Coach Calhoun's arrival.

Following the nearly four-hour practice session that included a sizable amount of suicide sprints, members of the media swarmed around Coach Calhoun and several Huskie players at court side for 25 minutes asking questions, both good and ridiculous.

When the reporters had their fill, UConn SID Kyle Muncy introduced us to Coach Calhoun. He was much bigger than we expected from television and although he had just spent most of the morning in practice and with the media, he patiently answered all of our questions.

Standing on the floor at Gampel Pavilion with the first few rows of seats as a backdrop.

Jim Calhoun Profile

BORN:

May 10, 1942

HOMETOWN:

Braintree, Massachusetts

HIGH SCHOOL:

Braintree

COLLEGE:

American International College - 1969

MAJOR:

Bachelor's: Sociology

Before the 2007 season, UConn had more current NBA players than any other school, a total of 14, edging out 13 Duke alums in the league.

Jim Calhoun Year-by-Year

Year	School	W-L (Pct.)	Postseason
1972-73	Northeastern	19-7 (.731)	----
1973-74	Northeastern	12-11 (.522)	----
1974-75	Northeastern	12-12 (.500)	----
1975-76	Northeastern	12-13 (.480)	----
1976-77	Northeastern	12-14 (.462)	----
1977-78	Northeastern	14-12 (.538)	----
1978-79	Northeastern	13-13 (.500)	----
1979-80	Northeastern	19-8 (.704)	----
1980-81	Northeastern	24-6 (.800)	NCAA (1-1)
1981-82	Northeastern	23-7 (.767)	NCAA (1-1)
1982-83	Northeastern	13-15 (.464)	----
1983-84	Northeastern	27-5 (.844)	NCAA (1-1)
1984-85	Northeastern	22-9 (.710)	NCAA First Round
1985-86	Northeastern	26-5 (.839)	NCAA First Round
1986-87	UConn	9-19 (.321)	----
1987-88	UConn	20-14 (.588)	NIT
1988-89	UConn	18-13 (.581)	NIT
1989-90	UConn	31-6 (.838)	NCAA Elite Eight
1990-91	UConn	20-11 (.645)	NCAA Sweet Sixteen
1991-92	UConn	20-10 (.667)	NCAA Second Round
1992-93	UConn	15-13 (.536)	NIT
1993-94	UConn	29-5 (.853)	NCAA Sweet Sixteen
1994-95	UConn	28-5 (.848)	NCAA Elite Eight
1995-96	UConn	30-2 (.938)	NCAA Sweet Sixteen
1996-97	UConn	18-15 (.545)	NIT
1997-98	UConn	32-5 (.865)	NCAA Elite Eight
1998-99	UConn	34-2 (.944)	NCAA Champions
1999-00	UConn	25-10 (.714)	NCAA Second Round
2000-01	UConn	20-12 (.625)	NIT
2001-02	UConn	27-7 (.794)	NCAA Elite Eight
2002-03	UConn	23-10 (.697)	NCAA Sweet Sixteen
2003-04	UConn	33-6 (.846)	NCAA Champions
2004-05	UConn	23-8 (.742)	NCAA Second Round
2005-06	UConn	30-4 (.882)	NCAA Elite Eight
2006-07	UConn	17-14 (.548)	----
35 Seasons		**750-328 (.696)**	

Coach Calhoun has had just one losing season - his first - while at UConn and has posted six 30+ win campaigns as the leader of the Huskies.

Interview with Jim Calhoun

What do you hope your players take away from their experience with you?

Calhoun: I hope that they understand that to be good at anything you have to accept working hard. That we set a precedent and standard basketball-wise, academically, socially, etc. You are going to have to work and no one is just going to hand anything over to you. So the moment you are not shooting a basketball for a living, and who knows when that is going to come, that you are going to have to settle in and work hard, and when you do usually good things happen.

You are already in an elite group with two, but what would a third national championship mean to you?

Calhoun: I think for us it is the desire to keep ourselves as one of the better programs in the country. I think we have been honing in on that over the past 15 or 16 years. We have had a lot of great things happen to us, a lot of great players, etc. So obviously the more banners you can put up, national championship banners in particular, and Big East banners, there is no doubt it enhances the reputation of the school, which in turn enhances the ability to recruit.

It is a self-fulfilling thing: if one thing goes well, then the other things go well. So as you win more, get on television more and quite frankly put more guys into the pros, all of those things eventually make kids want to play here.

From a personal standpoint, we feel that we have had a lot of teams that were capable of winning national championships, but the bottom line is that winning that national championship would be very special for any program.

Over the past eight years, we have won two national championships (99, 04), and any decade if you can win three or possibly four, now you put yourself in a unique category of schools.

With your successful battle with cancer, how has it changed your outlook on coaching and life in general?

Calhoun: It made me appreciate what I did, and it made me appreciate my family more. It was virtually impossible for me to appreciate

In February 2003, Coach Calhoun was diagnosed with prostate cancer and successfully defeated it, returning to coaching just days after surgery.

them more, because I have always been very family oriented. I didn't love the game more or less, I didn't love the kids (players) more or less, but I think it made me appreciate just how fortunate I was.

Here I am, 35 years as a coach. That is the one thing, my priorities have always been my family, my God, then my profession, so it gave me a chance to look around and say, "Hey, I have a pretty good life!" No question, it made me realize how fortunate my life has been, and how I have been able to have such a great family and have such a great job that I really, really enjoy.

If UConn goes 19-12 everyone asks "What is wrong with UConn?" As a program how is it dealing with the pressure of expectations?

Calhoun: When you have established yourself as a program of national attention, get some of the players you are fortunate to get, coupled with the kids' success in the NBA... When kids come to Connecticut, unknowingly or knowingly it makes no difference, there is a certain amount of pressure they are going to deal with.

The fans are used to seeing 30-4, and our fans want more. They want us in the national championship, but a minimum of a Final Four, and there are not too many programs that deal with the pressure of a minimum of a Final Four.

At what point in your career did you feel that coaching was for you?

Calhoun: I have never felt that way, and I don't feel that way today, the only thing I care about is this basketball team in front of me today. I really don't give an awful lot of thought, my motives may shift to recruiting, but with that said my mode might shift, and I don't even think about the past. I am just as anxious now as I was 10 years ago about doing well.

On draft night 2007, UConn product Ray Allen was traded to the Boston Celtics to help turn around the franchise. In 2007, Allen averaged 26.4 ppg.

Jay Wright
October 15, 2006

The trip from UConn to Villanova was interesting. The state of Connecticut and the Merritt Parkway has little service areas just off the side of the highway. Unfortunately, there isn't room for an on-ramp, they only have stop signs, and you're forced to find a break in the two lanes of traffic before putting the pedal to the floor and uttering a prayer, hoping not to get run over. Semi-trucks aren't allowed on the road but apparently that restriction doesn't extend to large dump trucks and delivery vehicles. Let's just say an accident was narrowly avoided on several occasions.

As darkness approached, we neared the city of Philadelphia. With Dave navigating and myself handling the driving duties, we were a little testy after the sub-freezing night in the car. We thought we had found a good route to Villanova north of the city, however, a lesson learned, always stick with what you know when it comes to interstates and highways.

At 7:30 on Saturday night, we arrived at our buddy Nate Wiecher's place. A Bowling Green alum and a big Detroit Tigers' fan, we showed up just in time to watch Magglio Ordonez hit a three-run home run to send the Tigers to the 2006 World Series. As long-suffering Cleveland Indians' fans, we were less than thrilled and headed to bed.

The alarm on my phone went off at 8 a.m. and by 8:55 we arrived to the 6,500-seat Pavilion on the Villanova campus, home of Wildcat basketball. Following Nate, a media relations intern at 'Nova at the time, we passed Villanova legend Ed Pinckney, who led the Wildcats to the 1985 national championship over Patrick Ewing and the defending champion Georgetown Hoyas, 66-64.

On the floor we found Coach Wright welcoming high school coaches from around the area to a morning clinic. We were supposed to sit down with him at 9 a.m. allowing us the time to make it to Syracuse for our appointment with Coach Boeheim. Unfortunately, a couple of things got mixed up and we would've lost the interview completely if not for

In 1983, Coach Wright worked as an administrative assistant for the Philadelphia Stars of the United States Football League (USFL).

the help of Nate and VU coordinator of basketball operations, Jason Donnelly.

At nearly 9:30, Coach Wright waved us over from the other side of the floor where he was seated near the baseline and led us to the adjoining media room nearby. We are not sure if Coach Wright ever knew of our project before sitting down with us, but he was very enthusiastic despite the early time and was very receptive to our endeavor. As he sipped his coffee, he really gave off a lot of positive energy. He needed to return to his clinic but he never made us feel rushed and was a very enjoyable interview.

He spoke about the battles that occur in the Big East when it comes to recruiting, but more so talked about the pride that each coach takes in the league and the respect that they maintain for each other despite the extreme level of competition.

We exited the media room and had our picture taken in front of the bleachers as the hundreds of coaches on the other side wondered what was going on. From there, we exited the Pavilion and headed up I-81 toward Syracuse

LED BY ALL-AMERICANS RANDY FOYE AND ALLAN RAY, VILLANOVA EARNED AN NCAA TOURNAMENT NO. 1 SEED FOR THE FIRST TIME IN SCHOOL HISTORY IN 2005-06.

THE BLEACHERS WERE PUSHED IN ON THE MORNING THAT WE MET WITH COACH WRIGHT INSIDE THE PAVILION.

JAY WRIGHT PROFILE

BORN:

DECEMBER 24, 1961

HOMETOWN:

CHURCHVILLE, PENNSYLVANIA

HIGH SCHOOL:

COUNCIL ROCK - NEWTOWN, PENNSYLVANIA

COLLEGE:

BUCKNELL UNIVERSITY - 1983

MAJOR:

BACHELOR'S: ECONOMICS AND SOCIOLOGY

COACH WRIGHT'S WIFE, PATRICIA (REILLY), IS A FORMER WILDCAT CHEERLEADER. SHE GRADUATED FROM VILLANOVA IN 1983.

Jay Wright Year-by-Year

Year	School	W-L (Pct.)	Postseason
1994-95	Hofstra	10-18 (.357)	----
1995-96	Hofstra	9-18 (.333)	----
1996-97	Hofstra	12-15 (.444)	----
1997-98	Hofstra	19-12 (.613)	----
1998-99	Hofstra	22-10 (.688)	NIT
1999-00	Hofstra	24-7 (.774)	NCAA First Round
2000-01	Hofstra	26-5 (.839)	NCAA First Round
2001-02	Villanova	19-13 (.594)	NIT
2002-03	Villanova	15-16 (.484)	NIT
2003-04	Villanova	18-17 (.514)	NIT
2004-05	Villanova	24-8 (.750)	NCAA Sweet Sixteen
2005-06	Villanova	28-5 (.848)	NCAA Elite Eight
2006-07	Villanova	22-11 (.667)	NCAA First Round
13 Seasons		**248-155 (.615)**	

The University of Rochester is where Coach Wright began his collegiate coaching career in 1984 as an assistant.

Interview with Jay Wright

What do you hope your players take away from their time with you?

Wright: Mostly, I hope they get to be the best players they can be and they learn how to be the best students they can be. Most importantly, one of my favorite parts of the job is that from the ages of 18-22, kids are tranformed from young men into men.

We talk to them all the time about learning how to excel at being a player -it doesn't matter if you are a pro or not - just learning how to excel and demand excellence from yourself, same thing as a person growing into a man, and same thing as a student. I hope they learn in those three areas about how to excel.

Coaching alongside some of the greatest in the game in the Big East, what is like for you from a personal standpoint?

Wright: It is a thrill, it really is. One of the things about those guys when you talk about the Pitino's, Calhoun's and Boeheim's is once you get into the league they are such good guys. I say this in a complimentary way, you lose the thrill of coaching against them once you meet them because they are such good guys. None of them treat you like they are legends and you are a young and upcoming coach. They are very respectful of the business, each coach and the league.

That is one thing you can really say about Calhoun, Boeheim and Pitino, even though Pitino came in the league late. Calhoun and Boeheim always did this, once you are a Big East coach there is a pride they take in the league and they treat you with great respect because you are in the league.

When Pitino came in he did it immediately because he was in the league when it started (Providence). As much as we compete against each other, and we do, it is vicious, there is a great respect level among all of us, and I think those guys set the tone for that.

In the last few years, after bringing the program back to the national spotlight, are you and the staff and players feeling more pressure?

Wright: It is funny because everybody from the outside asks that, but if you are on the inside they always expect you to be there. So there is actually more pressure at Villanova when you are there because they

Former VU star and current assistant coach Ed Pinckney was named the MVP of the 1985 NCAA Final Four. 'Nova upset Georgetown for the title, 66-64.

expect it, the fans expect it. Villanova was in the first Final Four in 1939 and multiple times since, and always has had a great tradition. There is a great pride in this program and there is always going to be pressure.

What do you feel has been your best coaching job?

Wright: It is hard to say, but our first year here, we didn't have any of the guys we recruited so that was the most difficult job we had. The system we came into was very successful, but it was a completely different style and system. So coming in and having to change the style of somebody else's player, it was very difficult.

By the end of the season, I remember Jim Calhoun said at the end of the Big East tournament, Ben Gordon hit a shot falling out of bounds with like four seconds to go, and if we would have won that game we would have gone to the NCAA's.

Jim Calhoun said that Villanova was playing as well as any team in the Big East, so we really took pride in that team.

But in 2005-06 our first recruiting class went through the system, and by that point they were rolling and it made it easier, believe it or not.

The turnaround success you have had at Hofstra and Villanova, what is your mentality when you take over a program?

Wright: When we were at Hofstra and came to Villanova I didn't think of it that way, but now looking back we did come in and take over two programs and got them going pretty good. When you are doing it though, you are just thinking this is my family, this is my home and this is where I am going to be. So let's build the family, build the program and every decision you make, you make it like you're going to be there forever.

I thought I would never leave Hofstra. I loved it and I still have a great tie to Hofstra. Same thing when I came to Villanova, you try to establish your foundation that this is a family, this is our life, this is my family, my wife's family, my children's family, this is the player's life, and when you become part of this Villanova team you become part of the Villanova family for life.

You try to get everybody involved in that and build a mentality that we take great pride in our program, and that is what we do.

THE LATE PAUL ARIZIN, AN NBA HALL OF FAMER, WAS CUT FROM HIS HIGH SCHOOL SQUAD AND DISCOVERED AS A FRESHMAN BY FORMER VU COACH ALEXANDER SEVERANCE.

Who have been your biggest influences in and out of basketball?

Wright: In my personal life, I would definitely say my mom and dad. My dad was always a coach and he coached me in baseball and football, but never touched a basketball in his life. So my dad taught me how to be a coach, and how to be a man.

My mom is such a great personality, she is just a character, and the way she loves people, and the way she treats people has been a great model.

Then as a coach, I would have to say the biggest influence is definitely Rollie Massimino, no question. But I worked for Mike Neer at the University of Rochester who won national championships and has been to Final Fours. Then I worked for Eddie Burke at Drexel University, who as a high school coach in Philly, is the only coach who has won the Philadelphia city championship at two different high schools - he was a legend. So I really have had great mentors.

Coach Wright was named Big East Coach of the Year in 2005-06, and was named America East Coach of the Year in 1999-00 and 2000-01 at Hofstra.

Associated Press National Players of the Year

Year	Player	School
1961	Jerry Lucas	Ohio State Buckeyes
1962	Jerry Lucas	Ohio State Buckeyes
1963	Art Heyman	Duke Blue Devils
1964	Gary Bradds	Ohio State Buckeyes
1965	Bill Bradley	Princeton Tigers
1966	Cazzie Russell	Michigan Wolverines
1967	Lew Alcindor	UCLA Bruins
1968	Elvin Hayes	Houston Cougars
1969	Lew Alcindor	UCLA Bruins
1970	Pete Maravich	Louisiana State Tigers
1971	Austin Carr	Notre Dame Fighting Irish
1972	Bill Walton	UCLA Bruins
1973	Bill Walton	UCLA Bruins
1974	David Thompson	N.C. State Wolfpack
1975	David Thompson	N.C. State Wolfpack
1976	Scott May	Indiana Hoosiers
1977	Marques Johnson	UCLA Bruins
1978	Butch Lee	Marquette Golden Eagles
1979	Larry Bird	Indiana State Sycamores
1980	Mark Aguirre	DePaul Blue Demons
1981	Ralph Sampson	Virginia Cavaliers
1982	Ralph Sampson	Virginia Cavaliers
1983	Ralph Sampson	Virginia Cavaliers
1984	Michael Jordan	North Carolina Tar Heels
1985	Patrick Ewing	Georgetown Hoyas
1986	Walter Berry	St. John's Red Storm
1987	David Robinson	Navy Midshipmen
1988	Hersey Hawkins	Bradley Braves
1989	Sean Elliott	Arizona Wildcats
1990	Lionel Simmons	LaSalle Explorers
1991	Shaquille O'Neal	Louisiana State Tigers
1992	Christian Laettner	Duke Blue Devils
1993	Calbert Cheaney	Indiana Hoosiers
1994	Glenn Robinson	Purdue Boilermakers
1995	Joe Smith	Maryland Terrapins
1996	Marcus Camby	Massachusetts Minutemen
1997	Tim Duncan	Wake Forest Demon Deacons
1998	Antawn Jamison	North Carolina Tar Heels
1999	Elton Brand	Duke Blue Devils
2000	Kenyon Martin	Cincinnati Bearcats
2001	Shane Battier	Duke Blue Devils
2002	Jay Williams	Duke Blue Devils
2003	David West	Xavier Musketeers
2004	Jameer Nelson	St. Joseph's Hawks
2005	Andrew Bogut	Utah Utes
2006	J.J. Redick	Duke Blue Devils
2007	Kevin Durant	Texas Longhorns

The first pick in the 1983 NBA Draft to the Houston Rockets, 7-foot-4 Ralph Sampson averaged 16.9 points, 11.4 rebounds and 3.5 blocks while at Virginia.

Jim Boeheim
October 16, 2006

When you have to travel 240 miles, find the facility and get to the interview's destination in less than four hours, it is nerve-racking. Those feelings are amplified when you are scheduled to meet with a Hall of Famer.

Once out of Philadelphia after meeting with Coach Wright, we were scheduled to meet with Coach Boeheim at 2 p.m. inside Manley Fieldhouse where the Orange were staging practice on Sunday afternoon.

At 1:35 p.m., we got off I-81 at Exit 18 and wove through the SU campus until we found Manley Fieldhouse at the corner of East Colvin Street and Comstock Avenue, passing the Carrier Dome in the process. It was just minutes before 2 p.m. and we couldn't find an unlocked entrance. After nearly circling the building, we noticed a door that looked slightly cracked. Desperate for a way in, we found ourselves in the kitchen and had to sweet-talk our way by a puzzled chef who was doubling as a security guard in our case.

We progressed through the bustling football offices and found a nearly dark arena, with pushed in wooden bleachers all the way around, lit only on the main playing surface, and inhabited by the Syracuse Orange men's basketball team who was just beginning their warm-up routine.

Looking like a pair of fish out of water wearing dress slacks and nice shirts, we walked in cautiously and stood courtside for a handful of minutes until Coach Boeheim, dressed in a blue and orange windsuit with a whistle around his neck, made his way across the floor and asked if we were the guys that had come to see him.

Despite practice commencing, Coach Boeheim never changed his calm and laid-back demeanor. At times he would blow the whistle, tell the players and assistant coaches what he wanted, move them along and then return to the afore asked question, in mid-sentence. He continued to speak with us for better than 30 minutes, going as far as to describe

Originally a walk-on, Coach Boeheim became team captain as a senior in '66 and alongside future NBA Hall of Famer Dave Bing, led SU to the NCAA Tourney.

where he acquired the Rolex on his left wrist. A gift from former Syracuse All-American and long-time NBA talent Derrick Coleman, Coach Boeheim said prior to receiving the gift that he had never had a good watch.

When Coach Boeheim started to blow the whistle more frequently and began offering deeper instruction, we eased ourselves out of the way and watched for nearly another half an hour. When we got the opportunity, we flagged him down once again and thanked him for his time and help before leaving the fieldhouse.

Before getting out of Syracuse, we stopped at the Carrier Dome, which frequently helps to place the Orange among the national leaders in attendance. We took opportunity to walk down on the field, which at the time was covered with new synthetic artificial grass. With the football field in place, it was hard to imagine a basketball game being played within the same venue. However, the Orange do, and more often than not they do it pretty well. Before long we decided to get back on the road as we had to attend class in the morning and still had more than 500 miles to get home.

The two days were exhausting but extremely productive as we ate breakfast with Schwab and met with three Big East coaches, two of which who are already Hall of Fame inductees.

After graduating in 1966, Coach Boeheim played professionally with Scranton of the Eastern League and earned second team All-Star status.

Just prior to the start of the Syracuse practice, evidenced by the whistle around Coach Boeheim's neck.

Jim Boeheim Profile

BORN:

November 17, 1944

HOMETOWN:

Lyons, New York

HIGH SCHOOL:

Lyons Central

COLLEGE:

Syracuse - 1966

Syracuse - 1969

MAJOR:

Bachelor's: Social Science

Master's: Social Science

The playing surface inside the Carrier Dome was named "Jim Boeheim Court" on February 24, 2002.

Jim Boeheim Year-by-Year

Year	School	W-L (Pct.)	Postseason
1976-77	Syracuse	26-4 (.867)	NCAA (1-1)
1977-78	Syracuse	22-6 (.786)	NCAA (0-1)
1978-79	Syracuse	26-4 (.867)	NCAA (1-1)
1979-80	Syracuse	26-4 (.867)	NCAA (1-1)
1980-81	Syracuse	22-12 (.647)	NIT
1981-82	Syracuse	16-13 (.552)	NIT
1982-83	Syracuse	21-10 (.677)	NCAA (1-1)
1983-84	Syracuse	23-9 (.719)	NCAA (1-1)
1984-85	Syracuse	22-9 (.710)	NCAA Second Round
1985-86	Syracuse	26-6 (.813)	NCAA Second Round
1986-87	Syracuse	31-7 (.816)	NCAA Runner-Up
1987-88	Syracuse	26-9 (.743)	NCAA Second Round
1988-89	Syracuse	30-8 (.789)	NCAA Elite Eight
1989-90	Syracuse	26-7 (.788)	NCAA Sweet Sixteen
1990-91	Syracuse	26-6 (.813)	NCAA First Round
1991-92	Syracuse	22-10 (.689)	NCAA Second Round
1992-93	Syracuse	20-9 (.690)	----
1993-94	Syracuse	23-7 (.767)	NCAA Sweet Sixteen
1994-95	Syracuse	20-10 (.667)	NCAA Second Round
1995-96	Syracuse	29-9 (.763)	NCAA Runner-Up
1996-97	Syracuse	19-13 (.594)	NIT
1997-98	Syracuse	26-9 (.743)	NCAA Sweet Sixteen
1998-99	Syracuse	21-12 (.636)	NCAA First Round
1999-00	Syracuse	26-6 (.813)	NCAA Sweet Sixteen
2000-01	Syracuse	25-9 (.735)	NCAA Second Round
2001-02	Syracuse	23-13 (.639)	NIT
2002-03	Syracuse	30-5 (.857)	NCAA Champions
2003-04	Syracuse	23-8 (.742)	NCAA Sweet Sixteen
2004-05	Syracuse	27-7 (.794)	NCAA First Round
2005-06	Syracuse	23-12 (.657)	NCAA First Round
2006-07	Syracuse	24-11 (.686)	NIT
31 Seasons		**750-264 (.734)**	

Through 31 seasons, Coach Boeheim has never had a losing record, and has been in a Final Four at SU in each of the last four decades ('75 as an assistant.)

Interview with Jim Boeheim

What do you hope the players take away from their time with you?

Boeheim: You get guys when they are basically 17 or 18 years old and you hope you can help them to mature, because to become a better basketball player you have to mature and become a better person on and off the court.

Guys come in and they are immature and there is a lot to learn in some cases, both on and off the court, and we are hopeful we can help them in both places. In the process, you hope they mature and become good people, like we try to do charitable things because we are the only game in town, such as Make-a-Wish, Coaches vs. Cancer, and they get involved with those, so that is what we are trying to do.

Having been at Syracuse such a long time, and only at Syracuse, who have been your mentors at Syracuse?

Boeheim: Well, I think in coaching you learn from everybody. I remember watching coaches do different things, from going to high school games, clinics or working at practices.

Coach K has helped me out a lot, as well as many others, and like I said, you learn from everybody, picking up little things from each coach. I think you are always picking up stuff here and there. We have a system here where we do certain things, but we will change drills and certain ideas each year to make us better.

Could you give us a quick overview on recruiting?

Boeheim: Recruiting is interesting. You are always trying to get the best players, but you are keeping an eye out for kids that will develop into the big-time players.

Everybody knows the top players and you are not likely to get those guys, I mean, we have gotten a couple of them over my 30 years, but not many. So we are looking for all types of players, but mainly the ones that will develop into pretty good players are the ones we really look at.

What was your reaction when you got Carmelo Anthony?

Boeheim: Well, when we first got him he was 185 pounds, so we thought he would be here for at least two years. He just got bigger right

In 2002-03, SU freshman Carmelo Anthony led the Orange to the NCAA Championship. 'Melo averaged 22.2 points and 10 rebounds on the year.

away, so he went from 185 to 220 in one year, so basically he put on thirty pounds overnight.

He was just so dominant, so physical, and if you have the type of year he had, there is nothing really to prove at this level. He was going to be Top 10 in the NBA Draft, so it was really an easy decision (to go pro). You just never know with players.

What has been your best team as far as talent, chemistry, work ethic, performance etc.?

Boeheim: We have had a lot of really good teams, so it is hard to judge one over the other. We won the national championship, so that is pretty good and in '96 we got to the Final Four and we were not very good at times. We struggled a lot during the season but that team pulled it together during the tournament. We ran into the Kentucky team, which was probably one of the last great teams we will see, so that '96 team was good.

We have had a lot of good teams and I have been fortunate to be a part of them. We want to be good every year but we want to be consistent every year, so I feel that we put ourselves in a good position each year.

If you had not won the title in 2003, what type of difference would that have made, ending your career without a national championship?

Boeheim: It would have been different; I mean it is important to win the national championship. I felt that I still would have had a good career, but winning the national championship is a big deal. It is a tremendous feeling for us, the fans, everybody, and all the players that ever played here. We really take pride in it, so no question it is very important.

The infamous 2-3 zone. Where did that originate from?

Boeheim: I played it when I was in school and Penn State used it against us, and it was good, and we used it when I was an assistant coach.

When I first started out, we played a lot of man-to-man, but the zone has become a good weapon for us and it keeps people a little bit scared of us when they come in to play.

Anthony was the 3rd overall pick to the Denver Nuggets in the 2003 NBA Draft. An All-Star in 2007, he has averaged 24 points through four seasons.

What does Coaches vs. Cancer mean to you?

Boeheim: Well, obviously it is important. We have all been touched by cancer, not only myself, but my friends, my family and colleagues. We have all lost a lot of people.

It is something as coaches that we have tried to do as a group because we have all been touched by cancer. It is a little bit about raising money but it is also about raising awareness for what people should be doing.

Is there a good basketball story you would like to share?

Boeheim: The one everyone tells is the one about hiring Rick Pitino on his wedding day, and the more I think about it, it is a funny story.

I got the job on Friday, and I knew about Rick and he was to be married on Sunday. I called him the day before (Saturday) and told him I needed to see him before he went on his honeymoon on Monday.

So I drove to New York and told Rick to come down to the lobby, and his wife, Joanne, kept sending the bellman down every 15 minutes, and we were there a good two hours.

The ironic thing is that they canceled their honeymoon. They came up to Syracuse and Rick and I went on the road and signed Roosevelt Bouie and signed Louis Orr, so that was a pretty good week. I don't know if I would do that (to Rick) today, but it worked out well for us.

In 2005, Coach Boeheim was enshrined to the Naismith Memorial Hall of Fame in Springfield, Mass. along with friend and UConn Coach Jim Calhoun.

Associated Press National Coaches of the Year

Year	Player	School
1967	John Wooden	UCLA Bruins
1968	Guy Lewis	Houston Cougars
1969	John Wooden	UCLA Bruins
1970	John Wooden	UCLA Bruins
1971	Al McGuire	Marquette Golden Eagles
1972	John Wooden	UCLA Bruins
1973	John Wooden	UCLA Bruins
1974	Norm Sloan	N.C. State Wolfpack
1975	Bob Knight	Indiana Hoosiers
1976	Bob Knight	Indiana Hoosiers
1977	Bob Gaillard	San Francisco Dons
1978	Eddie Sutton	Arkansas Razorbacks
1979	Bill Hodges	Indiana State Sycamores
1980	Ray Meyer	DePaul Blue Demons
1981	Ralph Miller	Oregon State Beavers
1982	Ralph Miller	Oregon State Beavers
1983	Guy Lewis	Houston Cougars
1984	Ray Meyer	DePaul Blue Demons
1985	Bill Frieder	Michigan Wolverines
1986	Eddie Sutton	Kentucky Wildcats
1987	Tom Davis	Iowa Hawkeyes
1988	John Chaney	Temple Owls
1989	Bob Knight	Indiana Hoosiers
1990	Jim Calhoun	Connecticut Huskies
1991	Randy Ayers	Ohio State Buckeyes
1992	Roy Williams	Kansas Jayhawks
1993	Eddie Fogler	Vanderbilt Commodores
1994	Norm Stewart	Missouri Tigers
1995	Kelvin Sampson	Oklahoma Sooners
1996	Gene Keady	Purdue Boilermakers
1997	Clem Haskins	Minnesota Golden Gophers
1998	Tom Izzo	Michigan State Spartans
1999	Cliff Ellis	Auburn Tigers
2000	Larry Eustachy	Iowa State Cyclones
2001	Matt Doherty	North Carolina Tar Heels
2002	Ben Howland	Pittsburgh Panthers
2003	Tubby Smith	Kentucky Wildcats
2004	Phil Martelli	St. Joseph's Hawks
2005	Bruce Weber	Illinois Fighting Illini
2006	Roy Williams	North Carolina Tar Heels
2007	Tony Bennett	Washington State Cougars

Ray Meyer, who died in March 2006 at the age of 92, led the DePaul Blue Demons from 1942-1984, winning 724 games in the process.

Dean Smith
October 20, 2006

Of all the trips, the one to Tobacco Road from October 20-22 posed the greatest amount of reward but also the greatest chance for disappointment. The idea of pulling off interviews with Dean Smith, Roy Williams and Mike Krzyzewski all in one weekend was a thrilling thought. However, as we made our way down I-77 late Thursday night and into the early morning hours of Friday, we had one meeting set up and the others were labeled as "tentative" at best.

After many patient months full of calls and e-mails to Coach Smith's secretary, we were able to secure a 15-minute time slot with the all-time wins leader at the time. His interview alone would've been more than enough to make the trip a success.

With the memory of sleeping in the frigid car in Connecticut still lingering in our minds, we checked into a hotel near Chapel Hill around noon where the outside temperature read 74 degrees.

Trying to thwart off any mishaps in transit, we left the hotel more than 90 minutes ahead of our scheduled time and headed toward the Dean E. Smith Center to meet Dean E. Smith, which was less than six miles from our hotel.

Once on the University of North Carolina at Chapel Hill campus, more than an hour early, we waited in the car and went over the questions one final time before entering the building and being directed to take the elevator to the basement where we would find Coach Smith's office.

The doors opened to the bottom level to reveal a plain, unassuming hallway. A few steps on our left we found a small office and soon we were conversing with Coach Smith's secretary, Ruth Kirkendall.

Ahead of schedule by a few minutes, Mrs. Kirkendall called down to Coach Smith's office and asked if he was ready for us. He was, so she led us from her office down a narrow hallway and at the end, we found Coach Smith's office and in the doorway to greet us was the UNC legend.

Wearing Tar Heel blue pants and a white North Carolina polo, he

In the United States Air Force, Coach Smith served as a lieutenant.

invited us to have a seat in his office, which was nothing like what you would expect. Approximately 8-feet by 15-feet, with no computer and minimally decorated, you would never know by looking at it that he had won two national championships and advanced to 11 Final Fours, second all-time behind Coach Wooden's 12 appearances.

Soon we learned first-hand that the dimensions of an office mean little to Coach Smith, nor do the records and accolades that he has garnered. Throughout the interview, he made it very clear that the relationships with his players and the lessons learned, both by the athletes and himself, far exceed the worth of the banners and trophies.

Coach Smith pleasantly answered our five handwritten questions that we had simply jotted down on a piece of notebook paper and expressed appreciation when we didn't attempt to take more of his time than requested. He informed us that many people ask for just a few minutes and then attempt to take much more of his valuable time.

Leaving his office, Coach Smith gave us a copy of his book - *A Coach's Life* - and walked us back down the hallway where he signed it and took a picture with us before disappearing back into his office.

Despite the huge victory, little did we know that our weekend was just getting started.

While in the Air Force, Coach Smith played and coached in Germany and then spent three seasons under Coach Bob Spear at the U.S. Air Force Academy.

The small reception area near Coach Smith's office in the basement of the Dean E. Smith Center.

Dean Smith Profile

BORN:

February 28, 1931

HOMETOWN:

Emporia, Kansas

HIGH SCHOOL:

Topeka - Topeka, Kansas

COLLEGE:

University of Kansas - 1953

MAJOR:

Bachelor's: Mathematics

Smith was named head coach at UNC in the summer of 1961 after serving three seasons under Coach Frank McGuire who left to become an NBA head coach.

Dean Smith Year-by-Year

Year	School	W-L (Pct.)	Postseason
1961-62	N. Carolina	8-9 (.471)	----
1962-63	N. Carolina	15-6 (.714)	----
1963-64	N. Carolina	12-12 (.500).	----
1964-65	N. Carolina	15-9 (.625)	----
1965-66	N. Carolina	16-11 (.593)	----
1966-67	N. Carolina	26-6 (.813)	NCAA Final Four
1967-68	N. Carolina	28-4 (.875)	NCAA Runner-Up
1968-69	N. Carolina	27-5 (.844)	NCAA Final Four
1969-70	N. Carolina	18-9 (.667)	NIT
1970-71	N. Carolina	26-6 (.813)	NIT
1971-72	N. Carolina	26-5 (.839)	NCAA Final Four
1972-73	N. Carolina	25-8 (.758)	NIT
1973-74	N. Carolina	22-6 (.786)	NIT
1974-75	N. Carolina	23-8 (.742)	NCAA (1-1)
1975-76	N. Carolina	25-4 (.862)	NCAA (0-1)
1976-77	N. Carolina	28-5 (.848)	NCAA Runner-Up
1977-78	N. Carolina	23-8 (.742)	NCAA (0-1)
1978-79	N. Carolina	23-6 (.793)	NCAA (0-1)
1979-80	N. Carolina	21-8 (.724)	NCAA (0-1)
1980-81	N. Carolina	29-8 (.784)	NCAA Runner-Up
1981-82	N. Carolina	32-2 (.941)	NCAA Champions
1982-83	N. Carolina	28-8 (.778)	NCAA (2-1)
1983-84	N. Carolina	28-3 (.903)	NCAA (1-1)
1984-85	N. Carolina	27-9 (.750)	NCAA Elite Eight
1985-86	N. Carolina	28-6 (.824)	NCAA Sweet Sixteen
1986-87	N. Carolina	32-4 (.889)	NCAA Elite Eight
1987-88	N. Carolina	27-7 (.794)	NCAA Elite Eight
1988-89	N. Carolina	29-8 (.784)	NCAA Sweet Sixteen
1989-90	N. Carolina	21-13 (.618)	NCAA Sweet Sixteen
1990-91	N. Carolina	29-6 (.829)	NCAA Final Four
1991-92	N. Carolina	23-10 (.697)	NCAA Sweet Sixteen
1992-93	N. Carolina	34-4 (.895)	NCAA Champions
1993-94	N. Carolina	28-7 (.800)	NCAA Second Round
1994-95	N. Carolina	28-6 (.824)	NCAA Final Four
1995-96	N. Carolina	21-11 (.656)	NCAA Second Round
1996-97	N. Carolina	28-7 (.800)	NCAA Final Four
36 Seasons		**879-254 (.776)**	

Coach Smith and Texas Tech Head Coach Bob Knight are the only two individuals to win a National Championship both as a player and as a coach.

Interview with Dean Smith

You do a lot to keep in touch with your former players, what lessons did you hope to teach your players over their playing careers?

Smith: That sounds kind of cocky, what *I* want to teach them, but I stay in touch because I care about them. All of those kids out there on the wall I care about. I mean you probably remember some of your teachers in high school or college that you stay in touch with while you are out in the real world.

We also get calls when people need something, like jobs or recommendations, so I pick up the phone and try to see what I can do. It is not something that I set out to do.

I do have one rule though. I go to their first wedding, but their second? No way. One of the first things Roy (Williams) did when he went to Kansas was he said up front that unless you guys get married in Lawrence, Kansas, I am not coming to your wedding.

After being competitive for so many years in terms of playing and coaching, how has it been stepping away from the competitive side of the game?

Smith: I know that I don't like it. I was always asked to do business talks or coaching clinics, and I did that for several years, and said this is ridiculous with all of the preparing, so I stopped that.

Other than that I get some competitiveness on the golf course. I go to (UNC basketball) practice. After my first year out of coaching I didn't even go to practice, but that is what I missed the most. I have more calls and visits with people than I did as a head coach. I didn't want to become busy, but now I am busy.

Who have been your biggest influences in and out of basketball?

Smith: As a player at Kansas, Dick Harp, the assistant - in fact Dr. Allen and Dick allowed me to put in some of the offense so they could concentrate on other things, so that was an influence that was important to me.

Bob Spear, the head coach of the Air Force Academy - I was his assistant for three years, and we would go watch film every night and our wives would wonder where we were.

In 36 seasons at the helm of the Tar Heels, Coach Smith's teams reached the NCAA Final Four 11 times, second only to Coach John Wooden's 12 at UCLA.

And my father was a head football, basketball and baseball coach in high school, so I guess all of those had a big influence on me.

In what areas do you think you improved the most as a coach?

Smith: I never thought about whether I improved as a coach each season. Although I assume that we do learn from each experience, and consequently improve. I do think I probably was a better coach after 36 years than I was the first year.

I was confident of getting our defense in gear the first year, as well as running a simplified offense, considering the personnel we had.

Each summer, when I took the family to the beach, I also took our film so I could study what we did the year before. And based on our personnel, what I could do to change for the better, whether it be offensively, defensively or, even more importantly, if we continued to rebound the basketball by blocking out defensively and by sending the right people to the offensive backboard.

Can you talk about your experiences with Michael Jordan at UNC?

Smith: Coach Bill Guthridge was the first of any of our coaches to see Michael play and that was in February of Michael's junior season. Bill thought he had tremendous quickness and was a hard worker who would be an ACC scholarship player.

Of course, we hoped his folks could send Michael to our basketball camp, which would give us an even better opportunity to determine if he was the kind of player we would like to have representing The University of North Carolina.

Our entire staff, Ed Fogler, Roy Williams, Bill Guthridge, and myself, did see him play frequently in the scrimmages at camp, but we were even more impressed with how he listened to the coaches to improve defensively, as well as offensively.

Michael was 6-3 at the time and had tremendous quickness. His competitiveness in a camp game was very obvious. Michael decided in the fall of his high school senior year to come to North Carolina. I know his parents seemed to be pleased with his decision, since Wilmington is reasonably close to Chapel Hill.

Mr. Jordan told us how Coach Driesell at Maryland kept telling him that the new bridge from Virginia to Maryland made it so the University

More than 96 percent of Coach Smith's letterwinners earned their degrees.

of Maryland was not much farther away than Chapel Hill. Mr. Jordan got a big laugh out of that.

Michael did start as a freshman in the first game against the University of Kansas. I started him simply for his defensive quickness and on how much he had improved defensively in our practices since October 15. We gave him a difficult assignment, and he stopped a 6-6 man from Kansas throughout the game.

As a freshman, he continued to improve and had some remarkable games, but was not quite as consistent as he would become as he improved each year he played the game. Michael also consistently beat his freshmen teammates to the loose balls that went out of bounds. Our rule was for the freshmen to chase the basketballs and reward the one who came up with the basketball.

Michael won the defensive award against Georgetown, in addition to swishing the winning basketball from about 15-feet to give our team the championship. When Fred Brown tried to pass the ball, Michael's defense caused Brown to hesitate and throw the ball right to James Worthy.

When the preseason All-America teams came out in the late summer and early fall, I was surprised that Michael did not get any attention as being an All-America as a sophomore. Ironically, without having any fanfare at the beginning of the season, Michael made National Player of the Year, along with Ralph Sampson, by the Sporting News. He was second in the voting in all the others.

Then, in his junior year, at the end of the season, he was the National Player of the Year, unanimously. He improved every year he played the game, even as a pro.

At the end of his junior season, Mr. and Mrs. Jordan came to Chapel Hill and I discussed what would be ahead for him as a senior. Mr. Jordan and I thought he would be selected very highly in the draft and, after calling a number of the people in the pros, Bill Fitch, the Houston coach, said that if they won the flip of a coin, he would take (Hakeem) Olajuwon, but if they lost the flip, he would take Jordan.

I then called Stu Inman in Portland. Stu said he needed a big man, so if he won the flip of the coin, he would take Olajuwon, if not he would take one of the big men at 6-9 and up, so he ended up taking (Sam) Bowie. In talking to Rod Thorn (who had the third pick with Chicago), Rod promised that if Jordan was there, he definitely would take Jordan.

In September 1986, the 300,000-square-foot Dean E. Smith Center was dedicated. It stands on 7.5 acres on UNC's south campus.

In talking with the parents, we then could safely say he would either be in Chicago or in Houston, if he turned pro. His mother thought he should stay and finish his degree first but, of course, Michael did finish his degree after going pro in the first two summers in Chapel Hill.

I thought he should go pro, only to avoid any injury. At that time, they did not have the big insurance policies that they now have, so we generally encouraged them to go pro if they knew they were going to be in the top five.

Coach Smith was named the ACC Coach of the Year on eight occasions - 1967, 1968, 1971, 1976, 1977, 1979, 1988 and 1993.

Roy Williams
October 21, 2006

Exiting the basement in the "Dean Dome" following our time with Coach Smith, we headed back up to ground level where the men's basketball offices are located. We tried to speak with UNC SID Steve Kirschner with regard to confirming a few minutes with Coach Williams on Sunday at ACC Media Day, which was the original plan of attack.

With a lot of open time before Sunday, we decided to find out Coach Williams' availability for Saturday, hoping to avoid the media day madness. Mr. Kirschner's office sits adjacent to the men's basketball offices and unfortunately, he was tied up for the afternoon with football issues.

We were just about ready to depart around 5 p.m. after waiting for better than two hours when Jennifer Holbrook, Coach Williams' administrative assistant, walked in and asked if we needed help. We gave her the brief project details which she remembered from an earlier attempt to meet with Coach Williams months before. Informing her that we had just met with Coach Smith, and that we were available all day on Saturday, she took my phone number and thought she would be able to talk with him and get back to us later that night.

Minutes after turning out the lights in our hotel room at around 9:30, my cell phone rang with an unknown number. It was Jenn calling to let us know that Coach Williams was available and willing to meet with us in his office in the morning before the start of camp. That phone call really changed the face of the weekend because we were leery of our chances of meeting with him at media day.

At 9:15 a.m. we found the door to the basketball offices unlocked. We entered the dark and seemingly vacant reception area and sat on a couch located near the 2005 national championship trophy. From another office popped Jenn, who was on her way to an event, and informed us that Coach Williams was just finishing a few things in his office and would come out to get us shortly.

Sometimes in meeting coaches, we were thrown right into the fire and

At T.C. Roberson H.S., Coach Williams lettered four years in both baseball and basketball and was twice named all-county and all-league in hoops.

didn't have that nervous period of anticipation time. In this case, things worked out beautifully. We waited for about 10 minutes in the office alone before a nearby door opened and Coach Williams emerged.

We shook hands and introduced ourselves as he showed us into his amazing office, which appeared in a commercial for Coca-Cola. He made us feel very welcome as he sat behind his large wooden desk while we each took a chair on the opposite side.

He is a great example of this entire experience as he didn't have the least bit of incentive to speak us, but still did and provided great in-depth answers as well as his undivided attention. As much as anyone, Coach Williams just fits. He looks, acts and conducts himself like the man whom you would expect to be the head coach at a program like North Carolina.

During a question regarding the 2005 national championship, which saw UNC defeat Illinois, 75-70, he took off his ring and handed it to us. It was absolutely stunning, a massive piece of jewelry with a large number of encrusted diamonds and the Carolina blue emblem donning the center section.

Following the interview, he gave us a picture-by-picture tour of his office. One in particular showed the before and after scene on Franklin Street, the main drag in Chapel Hill for students and fans of the Tar Heels. At 10:55 on the night of the 2005 title victory, the picture shows the street nearly deserted as the Tar Heels were putting the finishing touches on their first title since 1993 and Coach Williams' first as a head coach. An hour later, the same stretch of road is flooded with tens of thousands of celebrating Carolina faithful.

Other pictures included some from Coach Williams' years spent at Kansas as well as a shot including Dean Smith, John Wooden and himself.

As we made our way back into the reception area, we snapped a photo in front of the case holding the championship trophy, shook hands and thanked Coach Williams for his time and willingness to meet with us.

In 1968-69, Coach Williams played on the UNC freshman team for Coach Bill Guthridge, who took over the Tar Heels upon Coach Smith's retirement.

The 2005 national championship trophy is looming over Coach Williams' shoulder in the basketball office lobby.

Roy Williams Profile

BORN:

August 1, 1950

HOMETOWN:

Asheville, North Carolina

HIGH SCHOOL:

T.C. Roberson

COLLEGE:

University of North Carolina - 1972

University of North Carolina - 1973

MAJOR:

Bachelor's: Education

Master's: M.A.T. (Master of Arts in Teaching)

Williams began his coaching career in 1973 at Charles D. Owen High School in Swannanoa, N.C. - coaching basketball, football and golf.

Roy Williams Year-by-Year

Year	School	W-L (Pct.)	Postseason
1988-89	Kansas	19-12 (.613)	----
1989-90	Kansas	30-5 (.857)	NCAA Second Round
1990-91	Kansas	27-8 (.771)	NCAA Runner-Up
1991-92	Kansas	27-5 (.844)	NCAA Second Round
1992-93	Kansas	29-7 (.806)	NCAA Final Four
1993-94	Kansas	27-8 (.771)	NCAA Sweet Sixteen
1994-95	Kansas	25-6 (.808)	NCAA Sweet Sixteen
1995-96	Kansas	29-5 (.853)	NCAA Elite Eight
1996-97	Kansas	34-2 (.944)	NCAA Sweet Sixteen
1997-98	Kansas	35-4 (.897)	NCAA Second Round
1998-99	Kansas	23-10 (.697)	NCAA Second Round
1999-00	Kansas	24-10 (.706)	NCAA Second Round
2000-01	Kansas	26-7 (.788)	NCAA Sweet Sixteen
2001-02	Kansas	33-4 (.892)	NCAA Final Four
2002-03	Kansas	30-8 (.789)	NCAA Runner-Up
2003-04	N. Carolina	19-11 (.633)	NCAA Second Round
2004-05	N. Carolina	33-4 (.892)	NCAA Champions
2005-06	N. Carolina	23-8 (.742)	NCAA Second Round
2006-07	N. Carolina	31-7 (.816)	NCAA Elite Eight
19 Seasons		**524-131 (.800)**	

Coach Williams spent 10 seasons as an assistant under Coach Dean Smith from 1978-88. In 1982, UNC won the championship with then freshman Michael Jordan.

Interview with Roy Williams

What do you hope your players take away from their time with you?

Williams: I will tell you a story and hopefully that will give you the answer. I recruited Marvin Williams for three years and only got to coach him one. I felt very blessed to do that because he never missed a tutoring appointment, he was never late for a study hall and he never missed a class his entire freshman year.

While he was here only one year, he tried to do everything we asked of him off of the court as far as his academic side to get as much as he could. He didn't just lie around in his dorm room and show up for practice, so he tried to get something out of the academic side of things.

Then on the basketball side of things, he was the guy who could have been a Top 15 NBA pick out of high school who wanted to come to college but never started a game on our championship team. He ended up being the second overall pick, so what I wanted to get out of him was getting the best out of him academically and athletically, and when he made the decision to leave early I was all for it because it was what was best for him.

Generally, I want what is best for the kid, but also what he wants as well, which is not always the same... which is hard. I want what is best for them but it is hard to tell a kid to turn down millions of dollars even though it is not what I think he should do, so I also fight a little battle myself.

So I am hopeful after one or two years that they feel I did not short change them, and that I never put my own interests in front of theirs and that I cared about them, not just points and rebounds.

It is well known that it took Carolina multiple attempts to get you back from Kansas. What makes North Carolina basketball, as a whole, so special?

Williams: Coach Smith has built something here that no one has been able to recreate. Coach Wooden won more championships, and Coach K has more as well, but no one has been able to create an atmosphere like here of family structure, and have a guy who played here twenty years ago care as much about a guy who is playing here now.

What I have tried to do here and at Kansas, is try to continue that link-

On July 8, 1988, Coach Williams was named the head coach at Kansas, replacing another former Tar Heel, Larry Brown, who won the '88 title.

age from one group to the next, to the next, to the next. I tell guys that James Worthy helped recruit Sam Perkins and he helped recruit Michael Jordan and he helped recruit Brad Dougherty and he helped recruit so and so. It is the uniqueness of it that sets it apart from the rest of the programs.

A goal for most people is to improve themselves as people and professionals. Is there any aspect of coaching that you try to improve upon the most?

Williams: Every aspect of coaching. I think I am a much better coach now than I was last year and the year before that. Every time I speak, some of the questions other coaches ask me make me think and allow me to do a better job next time. No matter what the level, junior high, and high school and so on, I think they give you fresh ideas. I say that I want to be better everyday and I do believe as coaches we get better with experience.

For me personally, I get better each year understanding or trying to understand kids with pressures and different demands they have with the culture we have today. You have to work hard to understand what they are facing when they walk away from you, whether it is mom or dad, an agent, a girlfriend or whatever... I just try to prepare myself.

Winning a second national title would put you in particularly elite company historically. What would it mean to you personally?

Williams: It is strange, because when we won here when I was an assistant coach it was so emotional because it was Dean's first one, and people had criticized him so much for not winning "the big one". I just walked around the court with tears in my eyes.

And I told my son, if I was ever on the court while winning another one, I was just going to walk around the court with my arms up in the air and celebrate. Then it happened, and you can't prepare because you don't know what you are going to think or how you are going to feel. It was a great thrill for me as one of our former players, now one of my assistants, hugged me. It was a wonderful thrill.

Sean May in the press conference told everyone he wanted to be the first one to hug me, so those were the things that stand out. My son even asked, "I thought you were going to walk around with your hands up?"

At KU, four players were named consensus first team All-Americans under Coach Williams - Raef LaFrentz, Paul Pierce, Drew Gooden and Nick Collison.

You just can't plan anything like that because you don't know how your emotions are going to be.

In 2005 we won, and within a week we were losing not only the seniors, but four underclassmen too, so we didn't have time to enjoy it, and have time to sit back and say "Wow, that is pretty neat." In the fall of 2005 we distributed the rings at the first home football game. At first we were just going to have the players out there, but I said the coaches should come, too. That was September 19 and we won the title on April 4, and that was the first time as coaches that we got to sit back and enjoy it.

So if I am ever lucky enough to win another one, I would make sure to step back and enjoy it a little bit more because back in 2005, we came back here on Tuesday and had a celebration that night, I took my staff and their wives out for dinner and at about 10 o'clock we were all dead. Then at 6 a.m. the next morning, I met my assistant in the parking lot and went recruiting.

So someway, somehow, I would hope that if there is a next time, I would find some time with family and players and coaches to sit back and enjoy the accomplishment, because I don't think we did a good enough job of that last time.

In 2005, UNC was the first squad to feature four lottery picks - Marvin Williams (2), Raymond Felton (5), Sean May (13) and Rashad McCants (14).

NCAA Tournament Champions

Year	School	Year	School
1939	Oregon	1974	N.C. State
1940	Indiana	1975	UCLA
1941	Wisconsin	1976	Indiana
1942	Stanford	1977	Marquette
1943	Wyoming	1978	Kentucky
1944	Utah	1979	Michigan St.
1945	Oklahoma St.	1980	Louisville
1946	Oklahoma St.	1981	Indiana
1947	Holy Cross	1982	N. Carolina
1948	Kentucky	1983	N.C. State
1949	Kentucky	1984	Georgetown
1950	CCNY	1985	Villanova
1951	Kentucky	1986	Louisville
1952	Kansas	1987	Indiana
1953	Indiana	1988	Kansas
1954	LaSalle	1989	Michigan
1955	San Francisco	1990	UNLV
1956	San Francisco	1991	Duke
1957	N. Carolina	1992	Duke
1958	Kentucky	1993	N. Carolina
1959	California	1994	Arkansas
1960	Ohio St.	1995	UCLA
1961	Cincinnati	1996	Kentucky
1962	Cincinnati	1997	Arizona
1963	Loyola (Ill.)	1998	Kentucky
1964	UCLA	1999	UConn
1965	UCLA	2000	Michigan St.
1966	UTEP	2001	Duke
1967	UCLA	2002	Maryland
1968	UCLA	2003	Syracuse
1969	UCLA	2004	UConn
1970	UCLA	2005	N. Carolina
1971	UCLA	2006	Florida
1972	UCLA	2007	Florida
1973	UCLA		

In 1957, North Carolina defeated Kansas, 54-53, in the only triple overtime game in NCAA championship game history.

Mike Krzyzewski
October 22, 2006

We made an effort to meet with Coach Krzyzewski on a number of occasions that fell by the wayside, mainly because of Coach K's brutal schedule. Finally we got it set up tentatively for ACC Media Day at the Grandover Resort in Greensboro, North Carolina, on October 22, 2006.

After having the fantastic fortune of meeting with Coach Smith and Coach Williams on consecutive days, we were pumped at the possibility of meeting the third major coach in the UNC/Duke rivalry, and come on, it was Coach K!

The event places all 12 ACC coaches in a large ballroom and gives each a roundtable at which media can come and go as they wish. At 11:45 a.m. the coaches made their way to their seats and began fielding questions until 2 p.m. Throughout the two and a half hours, Coach Williams and Coach K were constantly swarmed by no less than 15 members of the media at a time. To help alleviate congestion, we're guessing, the two were seated on opposite sides of the room.

With their tables full, we took advantage of the opportunity and had the chance to listen and briefly speak with several other ACC coaches, including Clemson's Oliver Purnell, Virginia Tech lead man Seth Greenberg and Paul Hewitt of Georgia Tech.

While the coaches were downstairs with the print media, the selected players present from each school were upstairs dealing with interviews from television and radio outlets. In speaking with Duke SID Jon Jackson, it appeared that Coach K would get a period of freedom during the transition from print to broadcast media at 2 p.m.

When the transition time came, we followed Jon and Coach K out into the lobby area and waited as Coach K spoke momentarily with several other people. As he turned around, Jon introduced us, which was followed by the extension of a right hand and "Hi guys. Mike Krzyzewski."

In the context of college basketball, and even beyond that, it was like the President of the United States introducing himself. Of course,

On May 4, 1980, Coach Krzyzewski was introduced as the new head coach of the Duke Blue Devils - his first win came on November 29, 1980 over Stetson.

it is what a person does when meeting someone for the first time, but this was Coach K. He is a first ballot Hall of Famer, the face of college basketball. He has a section of the Duke campus named after him and his reputation extends far beyond the realm of just basketball. Nearly everyone, whether they like hoops or not, knows who Mike Krzyzewski is.

The four of us took the elevator upstairs to where broadcast media were conducting interviews and very luckily we found an empty conference room. There, we were able to speak to Coach K, just Dave and I, for better than 20 minutes before he had to get to other "official" media interviews.

Despite having just finished better than two hours of interviews and getting set for several more hours, Coach K offered good perspective on the life and responsibilities that he has as the most prominent figure in college basketball today. He didn't make us feel rushed, he didn't give us the corporate line, he didn't give us short answers and he put no pressure on us whatsoever. It can be intimidating talking to people like him, but he didn't bring out those feelings in the least.

Going into the interview we knew the immensity of his schedule, but it didn't become crystal clear until he broke down for us all of his responsibilities. The best of the best are no longer coaches, they're the face of college basketball, they're celebrities.

After Jon Jackson clicked the photo, Coach K shook our hands once more and returned to the feeding frenzy of the awaiting media.

With 10 NCAA Final Fours, Coach Krzyzewski ranks third on the all-time list behind John Wooden with 12 and Dean Smith with 11.

In an otherwise empty conference room inside the Grandover Resort at ACC Media Day.

Mike Krzyzewski Profile

BORN:

February 13, 1947

HOMETOWN:

Chicago, Illinois

HIGH SCHOOL:

Weber

COLLEGE:

United States Military Academy - 1969

MAJOR:

Bachelor of Science

(There were no specific majors at USMA)

Sixty-eight victories in the NCAA Tournament makes Coach Krzyzewski No. 1 all-time in that department, three more than Dean Smith's 65 at UNC.

Mike Krzyzewski Year-by-Year

Year	School	W-L (Pct.)	Postseason
1975-76	Army	11-14 (.440)	----
1976-77	Army	20-8 (.714)	----
1977-78	Army	19-9 (.679)	NIT
1978-79	Army	14-11 (.560)	----
1979-80	Army	9-17 (.321)	----
1980-81	Duke	17-13 (.567)	NIT
1981-82	Duke	10-17 (.370)	----
1982-83	Duke	11-17 (.393)	----
1983-84	Duke	24-10 (.706)	NCAA (0-1)
1984-85	Duke	23-8 (.742)	NCAA Second Round
1985-86	Duke	37-3 (.925)	NCAA Runner-Up
1986-87	Duke	24-9 (.727)	NCAA Sweet Sixteen
1987-88	Duke	28-7 (.800)	NCAA Final Four
1988-89	Duke	28-8 (.778)	NCAA Final Four
1989-90	Duke	29-9 (.763)	NCAA Runner-Up
1990-91	Duke	32-7 (.821)	NCAA Champions
1991-92	Duke	34-2 (.944)	NCAA Champions
1992-93	Duke	24-8 (.750)	NCAA Second Round
1993-94	Duke	28-6 (.824)	NCAA Runner-Up
1994-95	Duke	9-3*** (.750)	----
1995-96	Duke	18-13 (.581)	NCAA First Round
1996-97	Duke	24-9 (.727)	NCAA Second Round
1997-98	Duke	32-4 (.889)	NCAA Elite Eight
1998-99	Duke	37-2 (.949)	NCAA Runner-Up
1999-00	Duke	29-5 (.853)	NCAA Sweet Sixteen
2000-01	Duke	35-4 (.897)	NCAA Champions
2001-02	Duke	31-4 (.886)	NCAA Sweet Sixteen
2002-03	Duke	26-7 (.788)	NCAA Sweet Sixteen
2003-04	Duke	31-6 (.838)	NCAA Final Four
2004-05	Duke	27-6 (.818)	NCAA Sweet Sixteen
2005-06	Duke	32-4 (.889)	NCAA Sweet Sixteen
2006-07	Duke	22-11 (.667)	NCAA First Round
32 Seasons		**775-261 (.748)**	

***After coaching the first 12 games in 1994-95, Coach K exited for the rest of the season, suffering with a bad back, surgery and exhaustion.

Interview with Mike Krzyzewski

During our discussion before the interview, Coach K offered his thoughts on why college basketball is so special.

Krzyzewski: College basketball is the most intimate of the big-time sports because we are dealing with a smaller number of guys that you have to build a relationship with. Not to take away from football, but you can't have that intimate relationship with 80-100 guys. But we have it with all of our guys, whether it is 11 or 12 and even with the managers...it is a neat thing. We play in our underwear, we don't wear helmets so we get to see everyone, and the intimacy just comes down to people.

Overall recruiting process, can you take us from identifying needs to actually signing the players?

Krzyzewski: You need good players and you need good kids. We never look at "we need a big guy or only need a guard" and that is why I don't position my kids. I am in constant search for kids that fit a certain mold.

First, they have to be talented to play and succeed at our level. Two, they have to be strong academically so they are not struggling at Duke and three, they have to have great character - good kids that already respect people and the game. So I am always looking for those types of players, no matter what position, because in college basketball you don't have to have a specific position, obviously you have to have a point guard, but you know what I am saying.

We are just trying to get good guys, so it is hardly ever about a need. It is just always pursuing kids who fit that mold, and then seeing if we have a skill set that fits his needs. That is why my kids play multiple positions, our offense and defense is set up that way.

How do you approach building such a tight Duke family year in and year out with kids coming and going and kids from different backgrounds and even different countries?

Krzyzewski: It used to be that you would change accordingly to what has happened out there, but basically what you are talking about is culture, and how do you perpetuate a culture that has proven to be pretty good? The outside has changed, the outside being guys leave early, so

UNLV pounded Duke on April 2, 1990 to win the National Championship by a margin of 30 points, 103-73.

our culture used to be taught to freshman by juniors and seniors, and then they became kind of like a fraternity.

Well all of a sudden, this year I have one junior and no seniors, or some of the seniors are not better than the freshman, so will the freshmen listen to a senior? So we have to look at our assistants being more involved with developing relationships, we've tried to develop relationships even closer with our recruits, especially once they commit during the year. Not that you wouldn't have a good relationship, obviously if they have committed to you, you have a good relationship, but you talk to them even more than you would have with a kid who signed 10 years ago because you knew that they were going to come in. You have a summer program where a kid comes in for a semester just before the start of school, so you are trying to get your values and standards already in their minds before they ever get here.

Could you take us through a day in the life of Coach K?

Krzyzewski: I can't do that because I'm going all the time. The thing that is so difficult is the amount of people that want information from you. Whether it is something like this, what you guys are doing, information on how to raise money, it demands so much and you would be shocked, you would be shocked.

I am president of the NABC Foundation, so we opened up the college basketball Hall of Fame, which starts this year - what does that mean? It means a lot. It means that I might have to make calls, write letters, or be on conference calls.

My daughter and I just wrote a book: what does that mean? I am coach of the US team: what does that mean? I am on the V Foundation: what does that mean? I speak: what does that mean?

Then, because you are on TV and have been there a long time, what do you do with the thousands of letters that people send you? The letter from a mother that says her kid is having a tough time in school, will you write my kid? Well, you do. Or the letter that says my father has just been diagnosed with cancer, could you call or write him? So you might do one or both of those.

All of those things are good, they are great, but then I think you guys are interviewing me because I coach basketball. There has to be a time if you are two of my players, we have to sit down like this and develop a

THE FOLLOWING SEASON, IN THE NATIONAL SEMIFINALS, DUKE AVENGED THE LOSS TO UNLV, 79-77, AND THEN DEFEATED KANSAS, 72-65, FOR THE NATIONAL CHAMPIONSHIP.

relationship.

Trying to do all of that, you need Jon Jackson, and people like that all around you, managers and assistants. That is kind of a full day, and they are rewarding days, and they are never the same. Not only do you have to run the basketball program, you have to be really good at it, I mean really good.

I go back to the first question when we talked about recruiting good kids. For the most part, I don't get surprised with problems; you won't have a bad attitude, that doesn't mean you won't be less confident at times. But my players, they deserve all the time I can give them, and they hardly ever put me in the position where you feel like "How could you do that?" or that type of thing. So it is about that too, surrounding yourself with good people.

Through this project, Jay Bilas has helped us enormously. Can you talk about one of your first groups of players and your first Final Four in 1986 and what those guys mean to you?

Krzyzewski: You talk about Jay Bilas, he was one of the Founding Fathers, so to speak, and so that group will always be special to me: Johnny Dawkins, Mark Alarie, David Henderson, and Jay. Those four kids were terrific... I would have taken that team anywhere.

That team, in addition to those guys, had Tommy Amaker (head coach at Harvard), Quin Snyder (head coach of NBDL's Austin Toros), Billy King (Philadelphia 76ers President and GM), Danny Ferry (Cleveland Cavaliers GM) - you talk about great people.

What Jay is doing (ESPN analyst), Johnny is my associate, Mark Alarie is in business... you can't beat that. Their group, as a unit they were as unified as any team could be, and that is why they won 37 games. Adversity unified them because they had only won 11 when they were freshmen.

In the summer of 1992, Coach Krzyzewski worked as an assistant with the United States Olympic "Dream Team" which won gold in Barcelona, Spain.

The Duke/North Carolina Rivalry...

Overall Series Record:
North Carolina leads 127-96 (.569)

First Game:
January 24, 1920 -- UNC 36 Duke 25

Decade-by-Decade Results:

1920s: UNC, 18-4	1930s: Duke, 12-10
1940s: UNC, 14-12	1950s: Tied, 14-14
1960s: Duke, 14-12	1970s: UNC, 23-8
1980s: UNC, 16-9	1990s: UNC, 14-10
2000s: Duke, 13-6	

Biggest UNC Victory: 55-18 - March 5, 1921
Biggest Duke Victory: 104-69 - February 29, 1964

@ Cameron Indoor: Duke leads, 38-32
@ Dean E. Smith Center: UNC leads, 13-9

Dean Smith Against the Blue Devils:
--Overall: 59-35 (.628)
--Between 1972 and 1977, Coach Smith won 17 of 18 contests against Duke.

Mike Krzyzewski Against the Tar Heels:
--Overall: 31-32 (.492)
--Since the start of the 1999 season, Coach K and the Blue Devils are 16-6 (.727) against UNC.

Roy Williams Against the Blue Devils:
--Overall: 4-4 (.500)
--After losing his first three games against Duke, Coach Williams and the Tar Heels have emerged victorious in four of their last five.

Dr. James A. Naismith was born on November 6, 1861 near the town of Almonte, Ontario, Canada.

Gary Williams
October 22, 2006

We got an absolute steal with regard to meeting with Maryland's Gary Williams. We had anticipated driving to College Park, Maryland to meet with the 2002 national championship coach at a later date.

Upon talking to SID Jason Yamin, who was handling the Terrapin media relations during the ACC gathering, he honored our request and said, "Why not just try and talk to him here and save yourselves a bunch of miles and another trip?"

We obviously agreed with his logic and after wrapping up our time with Coach Krzyzewski, we went back to the hallway and found Coach Williams sitting on a nearby bench waiting for his series of television and radio interviews to commence.

He had been briefed about what we were looking to do and he was very open to talking with us, but there just was one glitch - he was "on call" for multiple broadcast media spots, thus we never knew how much time we were going to have with each exchange. When Coach Williams was called away, he would enter a room while we stayed outside and a few minutes later he would return and pick up where we had left off.

Sometimes we were able to get in one question, sometimes we had to start again from scratch. Afraid that the back and forth nature of the interview was going to quickly become annoying for Coach Williams, we eliminated several of our questions, and the picture that you'll see several pages later is located in front one of the media rooms on the upstairs level inside the Grandover Resort.

Quite possibly the atmosphere around the event had something to do with it, but Coach Williams, a Maryland alum himself, made it difficult for us at times to determine whether he was being serious or joking with us. Each time that he returned from a television or radio session he would tell us about it, whether the reporter was good, bad, goofy or however else.

When we asked him about his best coaching job, we suspected his response might be the 2002 season when Juan Dixon, Steve Blake, Lonny

Coach Williams lettered as a Terrapin from 1965-67 playing the point guard position. He was the team captain as a senior.

Baxter and Chris Wilcox led the Terrapins to a 32-4 record and the national championship. Instead he credited his fourth season, way back in 1993-94 when Maryland went 18-12 and advanced to the Sweet Sixteen after having missed the postseason through his first three campaigns in College Park.

Since those initial three years, 1991-93, when Maryland went 42-43 with no postseason berths, the 1968 UM alum has posted a record of 317-143, and has taken the Terps to either the NCAA or NIT in 14 consecutive seasons, including a Final Four appearance in 2001 and the aforementioned championship season of 2002.

After completing our fourth successful interview in a span of three days, we knew that we had something special brewing. We view it as the turning point that played a pivotal role in the overall success of our project. All four coaches from that weekend possess national championship rings, more than 500 victories and are equipped with names such as Williams, Krzyzewski and Smith, all synonymous with college basketball.

A 1968 GRADUATE OF MARYLAND, COACH WILLIAMS RETURNED IN 1989 AFTER HEAD COACHING STINTS AT AMERICAN (4 YRS), BOSTON COLLEGE (4 YRS) AND OHIO STATE (3 YRS).

Upstairs in a large hallway inside the Grandover Resort before Coach Williams had to return to media duties.

Gary Williams Profile

BORN:

March 4, 1945

HOMETOWN:

Collingswood, New Jersey

HIGH SCHOOL:

Collingswood

COLLEGE:

University of Maryland - 1968

MAJOR:

Bachelor's: Business Administration

As the head coach at Woodrow Wilson High School in Camden, N.J. in the early '70s, Coach Williams led WWHS to a 27-0 record and the state title.

Gary Williams Year-By-Year

Year	School	W-L (Pct.)	Postseason
1978-79	American	14-13 (.519)	----
1979-80	American	13-14 (.481)	----
1980-81	American	24-6 (.800)	NIT
1981-82	American	21-9 (.700)	NIT
1982-83	Boston Coll.	25-7 (.781)	NCAA (1-1)
1983-84	Boston Coll.	18-12 (.600)	NIT
1984-85	Boston Coll.	20-11 (.645)	NCAA Sweet Sixteen
1985-86	Boston Coll.	13-15 (.464)	----
1986-87	Ohio State	20-13 (.606)	NCAA Second Round
1987-88	Ohio State	20-13 (.606)	NIT
1988-89	Ohio State	19-15 (.559)	NIT
1989-90	Maryland	19-14 (.576)	NIT
1990-91	Maryland	16-12 (.571)	----
1991-92	Maryland	14-15 (.483)	----
1992-93	Maryland	12-16 (.429)	----
1993-94	Maryland	18-12 (.600)	NCAA Sweet Sixteen
1994-95	Maryland	26-8 (.765)	NCAA Sweet Sixteen
1995-96	Maryland	17-13 (.567)	NCAA First Round
1996-97	Maryland	21-11 (.656)	NCAA First Round
1997-98	Maryland	21-11 (.656)	NCAA Sweet Sixteen
1998-99	Maryland	28-6 (.824)	NCAA Sweet Sixteen
1999-00	Maryland	25-10 (.714)	NCAA Second Round
2000-01	Maryland	25-11 (.694)	NCAA Final Four
2001-02	Maryland	32-4 (.889)	NCAA Champions
2002-03	Maryland	21-10 (.677)	NCAA Sweet Sixteen
2003-04	Maryland	20-12 (.625)	NCAA Second Round
2004-05	Maryland	19-13 (.594)	NIT
2005-06	Maryland	19-13 (.594)	NIT
2006-07	Maryland	25-9 (.735)	NCAA Second Round
29 Seasons		**585-328 (.641)**	

Williams is one of just 11 coaches in history to guide their Alma Mater to a National Championship, and one of only three dating back to 1975.

Interview with Gary Williams

What do you hope players take away from their time with you?

Williams: I hope they get better, obviously as basketball players, but also as people. You know, I think part of going to a university is to see more things, different people, and different cultures, like it is at Maryland.

What I want them to get overall is that there are a lot of good people out there, and there is not one way of getting things done. You don't have to be a certain way to be accepted by everybody. Those things along with a quality education is what I hope they take away.

What do you enjoy the most and least about coaching?

Williams: I really enjoy being on the practice court teaching because I think every coach starts out as a teacher. The demands now on your time away from basketball have gotten increasingly tougher with fundraising, speaking, etc.

Recruiting has gotten tougher because there are so many people you have to deal with now, it used to be just the high school coach and now you may never meet the high school coach.

If your career was over right now would you say you accomplished everything you wanted to?

Williams: As a coach you want to go on for a while but as you said health-wise or if somebody doesn't want you to coach anymore, that would cut it that short. I could walk away because I have coached at every level.

I started out as a junior varsity coach. I coached at American University when we didn't even have a gym. But it has been fun, it has been a good run. Now I hope I know when it is time for me to walk away, I don't want people saying, "He is limping around and cannot even get off of the bench anymore!"

What kind of pressure is it year in and year out playing in the ACC?

Williams: I think every game you play you could lose and that is the pressure of the ACC. If you look at teams one through 12, name a bad basketball program - you can't, they are all capable. Once you start in

Coach Williams has produced six NBA Lottery picks - Joe Smith (1), Steve Francis (2), Dennis Hopson (3), Jim Jackson (5), Walt Williams (7) and Chris Wilcox (8).

January there is no rest because two or three times a week you are putting it out there that you might lose.

People would probably consider the 2002 title team your best coaching job. What do you think has been your best single season coaching job?

Williams: I had a really good team that went to the Final Four the year before so I knew going into the 2002 season that we were going to be pretty good. So I just had to keep them playing the same way, it wasn't that I had to teach those guys a lot of things, or motivate them. We had three seniors on that team and we had to watch that quite a bit to stay together as a team.

About 14 or 15 years ago was the first year that we were really good at Maryland. We started two freshmen and three sophomores in the ACC, and we managed to get to .500 in the league and fight our way into the NCAA Tournament, and that was Maryland's first in a long time.

That might have been the best coaching job because we were teaching as we went through the season. It just wasn't getting ready for the next game, but it was about getting the players better over time, so I enjoyed that year a lot. If I had to judge myself, I would have to say that year.

In 2002, the 'Terps became the first team in NCAA Tourney history to reach the championship game by defeating the highest seeded opponents possible.

Mike Brey
December 15, 2006

A wooden gate across a road rarely spells good news. We encountered one on the University of Notre Dame campus in South Bend, Indiana.

Coming down Douglas Road with the university on the passenger's side, I was unsure of where to turn in order to get to the Joyce Center, the home of Irish basketball and Coach Brey's office.

Unfortunately, I pulled the trigger too soon. Approaching the aforementioned gate, I quickly realized that it was automated and would rise only for those with a special clearance pass.

There was a car in front, a car behind and students walking to class all over the place. With no legitimate place to turn around without looking like a complete fool, I got right on the bumper of the guy in front of us and plowed through behind him just as the gate was coming down. Dozens of students witnessed the brilliant move and the person behind us had to be shaking their head in disbelief.

Thankfully, after turning around, the exit gate rose when it sensed movement. Still, it was embarrassing and time consuming as we were trying to get to our noon interview with Coach Brey.

Finally, we arrived at the Joyce Center about 10 minutes ahead of time. Originally opening in 1968 at a cost of $8.6 million, the facility features a beautiful area that displays history from Notre Dame athletics, and not just basketball.

The arena itself is pretty dark and that will change in the near future as UND has a $24.7 million renovation planned for the aging facility. The capacity will be reduced from about 11,400 to approximately 9,800 but will allow for better seating, new private suites and hospitality areas. The renderings that we saw look absolutely incredible both inside and out.

As for Coach Brey, he was excellent as well. He is described as a "player's coach" and it was easy to understand why upon talking with him. We sat down in his office and got off topic a number of times

Coach Brey played three seasons at Northwestern State in Louisiana before finishing at George Washington in 1982.

throughout the 40-minute session, and that was a great thing. The best interviews throughout this entire project came when the coach was comfortable enough with us to get off the subject at hand. When they talked to us like knowledgeable basketball fans and not as 22-year-old kids.

Coach Brey took us all the way back to his high school playing days at legendary DeMatha High School under coach Morgan Wootten in the mid-70s. Early in his senior season he contracted mononucleosis and by the time he got healthy it was extremely tough to get his minutes back due to the vast amount of talent around him.

Still, he received two Division I offers and played three seasons at Northwestern State in Natchitoches, Louisiana, before transferring and playing his senior year at George Washington University in 1981-82.

Even though Coach Brey finds himself surrounded by the football craze of Notre Dame, he does a great job not getting lost in the midst of "Touchdown Jesus".

At GW as a senior in 1981-82, Coach Brey earned team MVP honors, was team captain and averaged 5.0 points and 4.8 rebounds.

Coach Brey's office inside the Joyce Center.

Mike Brey Profile

BORN:

March 22, 1959

HOMETOWN:

Bethesda, Maryland

HIGH SCHOOL:

DeMatha - Hyattsville, Maryland

COLLEGE:

George Washington University - 1982

MAJOR:

Bachelor's: Physical Education

From 1987-1995, Coach Brey was an assistant at Duke. During the time, the Blue Devils won back-to-back national championships and went to six Final Fours.

Mike Brey Year-by-Year

Year	School	W-L (Pct.)	Postseason
1995-96	Delaware	15-12 (.556)	----
1996-97	Delaware	15-16 (.484)	----
1997-98	Delaware	20-10 (.667)	NCAA First Round
1998-99	Delaware	25-6 (.806)	NCAA First Round
1999-00	Delaware	24-8 (.750)	NIT
2000-01	Notre Dame	20-10 (.667)	NCAA Second Round
2001-02	Notre Dame	22-11 (.667)	NCAA Second Round
2002-03	Notre Dame	24-10 (.706)	NCAA Sweet Sixteen
2003-04	Notre Dame	19-13 (.594)	NIT
2004-05	Notre Dame	17-12 (.586)	NIT
2005-06	Notre Dame	16-14 (.533)	NIT
2006-07	Notre Dame	24-8 (.750)	NCAA First Round
12 Seasons		**241-130 (.650)**	

Through the 102-year history of Irish basketball, Coach Brey is the only person to lead Notre Dame to three consecutive 20+ win seasons.

Interview with Mike Brey

What do you hope your players take away from their time with you?

Brey: I was talking with my wife about this the other day and the places that I have been both as an assistant and a head coach have been places where the combination of athletics and academics have been pretty intense, so there are great teachers all over campus.

If my players can say that the best teacher that they had at Notre Dame was Coach Brey it would mean a lot to me. Now I get the advantage of talking to them about life, and disappointment and intensity that the talented professors don't get the opportunity to talk about. Anytime your guys come back and say 'Coach, remember the time you pulled me aside and spent some quality time with me?' It may have not even been basketball, it could be that my brother was in trouble or my mom and dad went through a divorce.

So I think of myself as a teacher, I got started as a high school coach and teacher, I am the product of high school educators, so those are things that mean a lot to me.

Being from Rockville, Maryland how did you get to a place like Northwestern State in Louisiana?

Brey: That's a great question. I did not have a real great senior year at DeMatha, a great high school basketball program, with great exposure and a fabulous coach with Morgan Wootten. I got mono eight games into my senior year and really never got back into it. By the time I got back we had two other point guards there, one was Dutch Morley who went to Maryland and the other was Sidney Lowe, so you weren't getting your job back.

I really didn't get as much exposure so the only D-I offers I had at the end of my senior year were from Northwestern State in Louisiana and the University of Vermont. Two great schools and I visited both of them, but when I got down to Louisiana I got off the plane and it was beautiful weather. There was something about the South, and it was a chance to play so I decided to go all the way to Louisiana from D.C. to give it a shot.

I look back and if the coach wouldn't have been let go after my junior year and I didn't go back to GW, maybe I would be a high school coach

Before coaching at Duke, Coach Brey spent five seasons at his high school alma mater, DeMatha, with legendary Coach Morgan Wootten.

in Louisiana. It is funny how fate takes different turns.

How did the assistant job at Duke come about?

Brey: I was very fortunate that when I played at DeMatha there was great exposure for the players, a good reputation and a Hall of Fame coach. When I went back to DeMatha as an assistant, I got some of the same exposure.

Here was a young guy who worked as Wootten's right hand guy. Even in the summers when I was home from college, I would help coach the summer league so I was working on my coaching career before I got out of college. As soon as I graduated Coach Wootten got me a history teaching job. I coached the junior varsity, had my own team at age 22 and helped him with the varsity.

But everybody came through to recruit our guys and saw a younger guy that Coach Wootten would say, "Hey Mike, why don't you run the defense today?" So it was good exposure for me as a young coach, and I was fortunate that Coach K wanted a younger guy after he lost a young guy to the head coaching job at William and Mary who was supposed to be there (at Duke) for awhile.

So Coach K didn't want a young guy who was going to be there for a couple of years and then move on to a head job. I was young, and I was going to be with them, and I was going to be passionate and enthusiastic. He felt he could train me, so I ended up spending eight years there, eight great years.

Was there ever a time you considered making a career out of something other than coaching?

Brey: I never really did and my dad used to tease me all of the time when I said I wanted to get into education and teaching and coaching. He would say, "Why don't you get into business and get a real job?"

Early he tried to push me away a little bit but the dinner table conversation with two educators was coaching and teaching. The two greatest mentors in my life, as good as Mike (Krzyzewski) and Morgan were, were my mom and dad since I saw them teach and coach on a daily basis. Those were two huge impacts on my life. You just naturally follow that path, so I never really thought about anything else.

As the junior varsity coach and varsity assistant, Brey's DeMatha teams went 139-22 over five years and earned the *USA Today* No. 1 national ranking in 1984.

You are described as a "player's coach", how would you describe your relationships with your players?

Brey: First of all, I try to make it my players program, I do not want to be on the front of the media guide. I think I have a very low or manageable ego - my wife might disagree - but it is their program and I want to put them out in front.

Also, when they come to practice, I want them to get better and look forward to working with me in an upbeat manner. I coach from a positive reinforcement point of view, to make guys feel good. I am always concerned about guys' self-esteem.

That doesn't mean I don't get on them, but I don't embarrass them, and if we ever air things out it is in here (the office) or in the locker room, in more intimate settings. Maybe the biggest thing is that guys play freely for you, that they are not looking at the bench, but they have a freedom to do their thing.

I think they feel they can come in here, the door is open, and talk to me about things other than basketball. They can come in and talk basketball if they want but just to have the option. The communication is the key, and I have always prided myself on communicating with young people. As a head coach as I get older I will never get distant. I am paranoid about getting distant from our guys.

What are the coaching differences between the Colonial League at Delaware and here in the Big East?

Brey: Probably less time being able to devote to coaching in the Big East, because there is so much more that goes along with coaching at this level as far as being an ambassador to the university, the public relations and the recruiting is more intense here than it is at Delaware.

You feel afraid that you are taking more away from your team at this level and you can allow it to pull you in so many different directions, you can get away from the most important part. I think as you get older as a coach you understand how to say no to things better, and I think I have gotten better at that over the years. I think at this level there are more potential distractions than there would be at Delaware.

Being the head coach at Notre Dame and being in a conference like the Big East, can you give us an overview on your position?

In 1999, ND hired Matt Doherty instead of Coach Brey. A year later, when the job opened as Doherty left for UNC, Coach Brey was the man for the Irish.

Brey: The one thing about it, on a daily basis I am amazed at the power of this place worldwide. Notre Dame next to my name makes me better on a daily basis, and I am aware of that and very grateful and honored to be coaching here.

It is a very special place to be associated with. It is a very different place, and while I have been here I have cherished it. It is a great fit for me for how I have been trained and how I do business. Nothing has changed from the day I got here in 2000. You want to do business well enough so you can retire here.

There is no other coaching job that I aspire to. The intensity of our league and how that has changed is unbelievable and one of our great challenges is finding our niche here in the new Big East, but I am excited about it. It is a really unique setting because we recruit against the Big Ten and play against the Big East.

In 2007, Coach Brey was named Big East Coach of the Year, leading the Irish to a 24-win season, and an 11-5 mark in the conference.

Mark Few
December 20, 2006

Gonzaga University is located in Spokane, Washington, not far from the Idaho border. However, we ended up meeting Coach Few approximately 2,600 miles from the home of the Bulldogs in New York, one of the greatest cities in the world.

The Zags, their more well-known nickname, were in town just prior to Christmas in order to play Coach Krzyzewski and the Duke Blue Devils inside legendary Madison Square Garden.

We had arranged with the help of GU SID Oliver Pierce to meet with Coach Few a day before the match-up, originally thinking that it would be at the team hotel. When offered the opportunity to ride from the hotel to MSG on the team bus to watch practice, we jumped at the chance.

As we hopped on the bus around noon on Wednesday, December 20, we were mistaken by several autograph seekers as Bulldog players. Trying to explain that we were just guests, we made our way onto the bus and sat in the front on the opposite side from Coach Few as he finished his practice schedule.

Riding through the crowded streets of Manhattan, our vantage point allowed us to watch the fast-paced life and happenings of "The Big Apple" around us.

Following a 15-minute ride that only took us a handful of blocks, we exited the bus and waited as the players grabbed their gear. We easily could have been asked to wait outside for practice to conclude, but Coach Few motioned us in and paved our way through security as he said to the guards, "They are with me."

Riding an old freight elevator up to the playing level, we walked through the famous mid-court tunnel into the arena where 36 years earlier the Knicks' Willis Reed emerged for Game 7 of the NBA Finals despite a deep thigh injury. Although he scored just four points, Reed inspired the Knicks to a 113-99 triumph to capture the 1970 NBA Championship.

Finishing shoot around were the Charlotte Bobcats, and with them

Coach Few spent time at two high schools in Oregon as an assistant coach from 1986-89 before becoming the graduate assistant at Gonzaga in 1990.

was former All-American and Gonzaga product Adam Morrison. As Charlotte exited, Gonzaga took the floor to begin warm-ups while Morrison stayed to briefly talk with several former teammates and Coach Few.

While watching the action, we spotted ESPN reporter and WNBA announcer Doris Burke partway through the session, talking with several people in the stands. Before long, she approached us and wanted to know more about our project. Following a nice conversation, the former Providence basketball star informed us that she had interest in interviewing us on camera the following evening during the game from the sidelines, live on ESPN2.

After about an hour's worth of practice, the GU players made their way to the bus. However, Coach Few hung around to speak with us and told the bus driver that he was going to walk back to the hotel.

As we spoke on the sidelines with the man who has led the Zags to no less than 23 wins per season during his eight years, we sensed a certain calm about him. While we were not intimidated by New York City, it would be a lie to say that we weren't slightly on edge. However, Coach Few, who hails from a town of less than 4,000 people in Oregon, seemed completely unfazed by the madness of more than eight million people in such a confined space.

Finishing the interview, we asked Coach Few to take a picture with us and he suggested shooting it while standing at center court. It was the perfect conclusion to the morning.

The following night as Duke and Gonzaga fans sold out the Garden, we watched from our courtside seats at the end of the Zags' bench. Due to the game remaining close to the end we never made it onto television with Doris Burke, but nonetheless it was an amazing experience. The energy in the building was electrifying and the Blue Devils eventually outlasted Gonzaga for a 71-67 victory.

Fifteen hours after the game we arrived home in Oak Harbor, boasting a population of about 3,000, compared to that of eight million in the largest city in the United States. Talk about a culture change!

Few was named head coach on July 26, 1999, after spending two seasons as a graduate assistant and eight more as an assistant coach for the Bulldogs.

Center court inside the famed Madison Square Garden following Gonzaga's practice session.

Mark Few Profile

BORN:

December 27, 1962

HOMETOWN:

Creswell, Oregon

HIGH SCHOOL:

Creswell

COLLEGE:

University of Oregon - 1987

Gonzaga University - 1993

MAJOR:

Bachelor's: Physical Education

Master's: Athletic Administration

Coach Few was named the West Coast Conference Coach of the Year in 2001, 2002, 2003, 2004, 2005 and 2006.

Mark Few Year-by-Year

Year	School	W-L (Pct.)	Postseason
1999-00	Gonzaga	26-9 (.743)	NCAA Sweet Sixteen
2000-01	Gonzaga	26-7 (.787)	NCAA Sweet Sixteen
2001-02	Gonzaga	29-4 (.878)	NCAA First Round
2002-03	Gonzaga	24-9 (.727)	NCAA Second Round
2003-04	Gonzaga	28-3 (.903)	NCAA Second Round
2004-05	Gonzaga	26-5 (.838)	NCAA Second Round
2005-06	Gonzaga	29-4 (.879)	NCAA Sweet Sixteen
2006-07	Gonzaga	23-11 (.676)	NCAA First Round
8 Seasons		**211-52 (.802)**	

Gonzaga has won the WCC regular season championship nine out of the last 10 seasons. Since 1997-98, the Bulldogs are 108-18 (.857) in the conference.

Interview with Mark Few

What do you hope your players take away from their time with you?

Few: I hope we build a lasting relationship so that we can call each other for the rest of our lives. That is the main thing - they can count on me to do anything for them.

I would hope that it would be vice versa as well, that I could call them and they can pick me up or help us out. That is pretty much the bottom line of being a Zag.

What would you say your coaching style is?

Few: I am not really sure. I just try to instinctively play off of who I am, and try to communicate with our guys so they know where they stand. I try to be flexible.

We are going to try to devise a scheme on offense and defense that our guys can be successful in, and that changes every year. I am not afraid to borrow from people. If I see something on television two nights before and I liked it, I do not hesitate to put it in and use it. I always want to play a fun style of basketball. On the offensive end we want to be aggressive and push the ball so our guys can have a lot of freedom, because I feel those teams are the most difficult to defend.

What is so special about Gonzaga that has made you stay at a mid-major, why you don't ever leave Gonzaga?

Few: If you have ever been there, and once my coaching colleagues come up to Spokane and see that the situation is top-notch they understand, it is as good as any program in America.

The quality of life is great, and I am a big quality of life guy - I want to spend the majority of my time with my family, or I want to spend time in nature. I like to fly fish and get out in the mountains, so I have the best of both worlds in Spokane.

What was the turning point in Gonzaga's success that has elevated it into the national spotlight?

Few: There are several things, the first thing being that I have been able to keep most of my coaching staff intact the whole time that I have been here. We also continue to grow in all areas such as recruiting, a

The WCC Player of the Year has hailed from Gonzaga in every season since 2000-01 (co-award in '07), including Adam Morrison, the 3rd draft pick in '06.

brand new facility and how we travel with charters and private planes.

The biggest thing for me is that I am a competitor and I want to win. I look at what I have and what I have coming in and I don't want to go some place else and try to rebuild a place and try to build it up like Gonzaga. Why don't I just stay at Gonzaga and continue what I am doing?

In general, what is recruiting like in Spokane?

Few: We have to be careful, and we can get in on guys, but we have to pick our battles and make sure that we are not wasting our time. You have to see what kids have an interest and which kids will fit. It doesn't make sense to go after a kid who will not pan out after being away from home, and we want to avoid the transfer situation.

Television has been such a powerful medium for the rise of our program. We are on ESPN more than any team out West because the Pac-10 has a Fox deal. So we are on and kids in New York or Florida can watch us play on television and that has been huge, being on national television 20 times a year. I realize we are on late at night but that appeals to the kids and that is why we are at the Garden, to maximize our exposure.

It doesn't seem to happen very often, but what was the process of being a high school coach, to GA, to assistant, to the head coach at Gonzaga?

Few: It seems like some other guys are starting to borrow that idea. I think it is the way to go because it helps keep continuity in the program because I didn't come in and change the program. I hope to start seeing that more often, reward the people who have put in a lot of time, a lot of sweat, a lot of heart and give them a chance.

At one point everybody was given a chance. Roy Williams, Coach K, Jim Boeheim were all given chances. The one qualifier that drives me nuts is that "he hasn't been a head coach". At one point everybody had never been a head coach, Larry Brown and Dean Smith were not head coaches at one time. So I was lucky and I was blessed that I was an assistant and able to move up and take over.

We even have it in the contract of our guys, that if something happens to me, then they take over. I think that is the smart way to do it, reward guys who have been serving you for so long.

An All-American and national scoring champion in 2005-06, Morrison averaged 11.8 points for the Charlotte Bobcats in 78 games in 2006-07.

Bob Knight
December 27-30, 2006

From the start of the season, we figured our best opportunity to get to Texas Tech and meet with Coach Knight would occur over Christmas break from school. However, to start the 2006-07 season, he needed just 11 wins to surpass Dean Smith's 879 victories for most all-time in Division I.

During our stay in New York City, the week prior to Christmas, we received an e-mail informing us that we could potentially meet with Coach Knight right around the record-setting game against the Runnin' Rebels of UNLV on December 28.

We called and spoke to Randy Farley, the SID at Texas Tech, and soon had a tentative appointment set up with Coach Knight for Friday, the day after what could have been the record-setting 880th win of his illustrious career.

Soon we began to wonder how we would get to Lubbock, Texas, located about 70 miles east of the New Mexico border. Checking on every last minute flight, we found nothing cheaper than $743 a piece, not to mention the additional expenses of a rental car, gas, hotel costs and food. We decided that we would have to drive the roughly 1,400 miles each way.

On Wednesday, two days after Christmas, we loaded the car with the necessities and also enlisted the driving help of our long-time buddy, Justin Radsick.

Twenty-two hours and five gas stops later, we pulled into a hotel in Lubbock at approximately 4 a.m. During the last stretch of the drive, from Amarillo to Lubbock, you often could not see lights of any kind in any direction.

By 6 p.m. on Thursday we entered United Spirit Arena with our provided credentials and had the chance to meet ESPN writer Andy Katz and also met up again with Doris Burke, with whom we had spoken with in NYC the week before.

A sell-out crowd of 15,000 jammed into the beautiful facility on the

A 1962 graduate of the Ohio State University, Coach Knight played with legends John Havlichek and Jerry Lucas. In 1960, OSU won the National Championship.

TTU campus and just before the 8 p.m. tip we took a look around and reveled in the fact that we had a chance to be present for a monumental moment in college basketball history.

Unfortunately for everyone cheering on the Red Raiders that night, UNLV took firm control of the game and despite a late comeback effort from TTU, it wasn't enough as they fell by a score of 74-66.

We soon made our way into the media room for the postgame interviews with each coach. Nervous and unsure as to how Coach Knight was going to be following the loss, especially since he had a number of friends, supporters and former players in town for the game, we stood in the back corner. More so, we were concerned about the questions that members of the media might try to ask concerning the wins record.

Coach Knight followed UNLV head coach Lon Kruger, made an opening statement regarding the game and proceeded to calmly field a number of questions from reporters. Throughout the whole process of eclipsing the record, Coach Knight stood firm that each individual game was on his mind and not Dean Smith's mark. When asked about it yet again following the loss, Coach Knight politely reiterated that his focus was not on the record but solely on the improvement of his team.

With the defeat, we knew the odds of meeting with Coach Knight were not good. The next morning we got a call from Mr. Farley, confirming our suspicions, but he asked us to please hang around for a good portion of the day in case something changed. Unfortunately it did not. Late in the afternoon, following a final conversation with Mr. Farley, we began the journey home without meeting "The General".

Three days later, on New Year's Day, Texas Tech narrowly defeated New Mexico by the score of 70-68 to give the Hall of Fame coach his record-breaking 880th career win.

ON JANARY 1, 2007, COACH KNIGHT SURPASSED COACH DEAN SMITH'S ALL-TIME WINS RECORD, EARNING HIS 880TH VICTORY WITH A 70-68 DEFEAT OF NEW MEXICO.

photo courtesy of TTU sports information

Bob Knight Profile

BORN:

October 25, 1940

HOMETOWN:

Orrville, Ohio

HIGH SCHOOL:

Orrville

COLLEGE:

Ohio State University - 1962

MAJOR:

Bachelor's: History and Government

Coach Knight's youngest son, Pat, is currently on staff at Texas Tech and is slated to take over as the head coach when his father decides to retire.

Bob Knight Year-by-Year

Year	School	W-L (Pct.)	Postseason
1965-66	Army	18-8 (.692)	NIT
1966-67	Army	13-8 (.619)	----
1967-68	Army	20-5 (.800)	NIT
1968-69	Army	18-10 (.643)	NIT
1969-70	Army	22-6 (.786)	NIT
1970-71	Army	11-13 (.458)	----
1971-72	Indiana	17-8 (.630)	NIT
1972-73	Indiana	22-6 (.786)	NCAA Final Four
1973-74	Indiana	23-5 (.822)	NCIT Champions
1974-75	Indiana	31-1 (.969)	NCAA (2-1)
1975-76	Indiana	32-0 (1.000)	NCAA Champions
1976-77	Indiana	16-11 (.593)	----
1977-78	Indiana	21-8 (.724)	NCAA (1-1)
1978-79	Indiana	22-12 (.647)	NIT
1979-80	Indiana	21-8 (.724)	NCAA (1-1)
1980-81	Indiana	26-9 (.743)	NCAA Champions
1981-82	Indiana	19-10 (.655)	NCAA (1-1)
1982-83	Indiana	24-6 (.800)	NCAA (1-1)
1983-84	Indiana	22-9 (.710)	NCAA (2-1)
1984-85	Indiana	19-14 (.576)	NIT
1985-86	Indiana	21-8 (.724)	NCAA First Round
1986-87	Indiana	30-4 (.882)	NCAA Champions
1987-88	Indiana	19-10 (.655)	NCAA First Round
1988-89	Indiana	27-8 (.771)	NCAA Sweet Sixteen
1989-90	Indiana	18-11 (.621)	NCAA First Round
1990-91	Indiana	29-5 (.853)	NCAA Sweet Sixteen
1991-92	Indiana	27-7 (.794)	NCAA Final Four
1992-93	Indiana	31-4 (.886)	NCAA Elite Eight
1993-94	Indiana	21-9 (.700)	NCAA Sweet Sixteen
1994-95	Indiana	19-12 (.613)	NCAA First Round
1995-96	Indiana	20-11 (.645)	NCAA First Round
1996-97	Indiana	22-11 (.667)	NCAA First Round
1997-98	Indiana	20-12 (.625)	NCAA Second Round
1998-99	Indiana	23-11 (.676)	NCAA Second Round
1999-00	Indiana	20-9 (.689)	NCAA First Round
2001-02	Texas Tech	23-9 (.719)	NCAA First Round
2002-03	Texas Tech	22-13 (.629)	NIT
2003-04	Texas Tech	23-11 (.676)	NCAA Second Round
2004-05	Texas Tech	22-11 (.667)	NCAA Sweet Sixteen
2005-06	Texas Tech	15-17 (.469)	----
2006-07	Texas Tech	21-13 (.618)	NCAA First Round
41 Seasons		**890-363 (.710)**	

In 1976, Coach Knight's Indiana team went undefeated, 32-0, and won the National Championship. No team since has finished a season without a loss.

Denny Crum
January 18, 2007

It took nearly five months to get a time set up and arranged to meet with Coach Crum but it was well worth the wait. After retiring in 2001, following 30 years as the head coach at the University of Louisville, Coach Crum maintains an office in the Alumni Center located on-campus.

We got to Louisville for a mid-day time slot and found a seat in the lobby on the second floor of the bustling building. Coach Crum's longtime secretary Judy Cowgill was out that day, however, another nice lady offered her assistance and called the veteran coach to inform him that we had made it down to U of L.

Soon, he walked into the lobby and introduced himself. Originally we stopped at a large conference room, but we exited as quickly as we entered and proceeded around the corner and down the hallway as he decided to conduct the interview in his office. His area, which wasn't huge, superbly painted a picture of his career with the Cardinals. With a number of pictures and mementos encompassing the office, the stories seemed to pulsate throughout.

The word warm is often thrown about with reckless abandon. However, Coach Crum was warm in every sense of the word. A guy who would be great to attend a baseball game with and sit in the bleachers, relax and talk about life.

Toward the end of our 45-minute session, he asked us if we had met with Coach Wooden. At the time, we possessed Coach Wooden's phone number, however, we were very reluctant to call and bother him.

Without batting an eye, Coach Crum went to his enormous collection of neatly arranged phone numbers and contact information. Before we could comprehend exactly what was going on, Coach Crum, a former UCLA player under Coach Wooden, was conversing on the phone with the legend himself.

Speaking for a few minutes about Coach Wooden's family and his recent goings on, Coach Crum then mentioned our endeavor and that we

Coach Crum played two seasons at Pierce Junior College from 1954-56. He scored 27 ppg. as a freshman and was league Player of the Year as a sophomore.

would very much like to fly out to California to meet the former UCLA coach.

When he got off the phone, we were in awe of what had just happened. Coach Crum silently pulled out a note card and wrote down Coach Wooden's home phone number. He then instructed us to call after departing his office, tell Coach Wooden more about the project and assured us that he would meet with us, no question about it.

Before leaving, Coach Crum offered to sign the copy of his book - *The State of the Game* - which I had brought along. He was done working for the day and decided to walk out to the car with us. In the parking lot we shook hands a final time and he proceeded to drive away in one of the largest luxury cars that I have ever seen! I guess it is one of the perks for having been one of the best coaches in the game for three decades.

Playing at UCLA for Coach Wooden for his final two seasons, Coach Crum averaged 7.1 ppg. from 1956-58 for the Bruins.

In the alumni building on the U of L campus
where Coach Crum's office is now located.

Denny Crum Profile

BORN:

March 2, 1937

HOMETOWN:

San Fernando, California

HIGH SCHOOL:

San Fernando

COLLEGE:

UCLA - 1958

MAJOR:

Bachelor's: Mathematics

From 1968-1971, Coach Crum was the top assistant for Coach John Wooden at UCLA and served as the top recruiter for the "Wizard of Westwood".

Denny Crum Year-by-Year

Year	School	W-L (Pct.)	Postseason
1971-72	Louisville	26-5 (.839)	NCAA Final Four
1972-73	Louisville	23-7 (.767)	NIT
1973-74	Louisville	21-7 (.750)	NCAA (0-2)
1974-75	Louisville	28-3 (.903)	NCAA Final Four
1975-76	Louisville	20-8 (.714)	NIT
1976-77	Louisville	21-7 (.750)	NCAA (0-1)
1977-78	Louisville	23-7 (.767)	NCAA (1-1)
1978-79	Louisville	24-8 (.750)	NCAA (1-1)
1979-80	Louisville	33-3 (.917)	NCAA Champions
1980-81	Louisville	21-9 (.700)	NCAA (0-1)
1981-82	Louisville	23-10 (.697)	NCAA Final Four
1982-83	Louisville	32-4 (.889)	NCAA Final Four
1983-84	Louisville	24-11 (.686)	NCAA (2-1)
1984-85	Louisville	19-18 (.514)	NIT
1985-86	Louisville	32-7 (.821)	NCAA Champions
1986-87	Louisville	18-14 (.563)	----
1987-88	Louisville	24-11 (.686)	NCAA Sweet Sixteen
1988-89	Louisville	24-9 (.727)	NCAA Sweet Sixteen
1989-90	Louisville	27-8 (.771)	NCAA Second Round
1990-91	Louisville	14-16 (.467)	----
1991-92	Louisville	19-11 (.633)	NCAA Second Round
1992-93	Louisville	22-9 (.710)	NCAA Sweet Sixteen
1993-94	Louisville	28-6 (.824)	NCAA Sweet Sixteen
1994-95	Louisville	19-14 (.576)	NCAA First Round
1995-96	Louisville	22-12 (.647)	NCAA Sweet Sixteen
1996-97	Louisville	26-9 (.743)	NCAA Elite Eight
1997-98	Louisville	12-20 (.375)	----
1998-99	Louisville	19-11 (.633)	NCAA First Round
1999-00	Louisville	19-12 (.613)	NCAA First Round
2000-01	Louisville	12-19 (.387)	----
30 Seasons		**675-295 (.696)**	

Crum was nicknamed "Cool Hand Luke" for his calm under fire by analyst and former coach Al McGuire.

Interview with Denny Crum

What is your hope that your players took away from their experience with you?

Crum: With life you always have adversity, so there are always things that come up that get in your way, so I think that is one thing. You want your kids to learn about being on time, about the discipline of how you treat your body in terms of what you put in it because you are what you eat and drink.

You want the kids to understand that basketball isn't an end to everything. It is a means for some to make a living, but for others it is just the enjoyment of competing. You have to learn to compete in life since you are always competing for jobs and positions and other things, and you have to learn to deal with that. You have to teach them how to prepare and see the big picture instead of the individual little things that people put a great amount of importance on. But really, in the scheme of life, they are not that important. You want to teach them how to respect other people.

I think the kids that have a chance to play team sports probably get as much or more out of them than anyone. They have a big edge over anyone who goes to college that doesn't have to compete against others, other than grades. You have to learn to get along and you have to learn to accept defeat. You don't have to like it, but you have to learn to accept it in a gentlemanly way, and learn how to win in a gentlemanly way.

You don't learn to win and then gloat to your opponent - you have to be a gentleman in both winning and losing. People who have an opportunity to compete in team sports, I think those are by-products of team sports that give them a huge leg up when it comes to living life.

Where did your red jacket originate?

Crum: Well it is our school color, and one, I always felt like it stood out on television. If potential recruits were watching they would remember you, so that you can wear that when you go recruiting, and they would recognize that you had been on TV because you stood out.

Have things like horseracing, poker, fishing and hunting been enough to quench your competitive desire?

On May 9, 1994, Coach Crum was inducted into the Naismith Memorial Basketball Hall of Fame in Springfield, Mass.

Crum: Those are the things that I do for that competitive desire because when you grow up in athletics you are cometing all of your life and it is hard to just turn that off. You can compete in fishing and in horseracing. I mean, it doesn't matter what you are doing, for me, I compete at everything I do. I don't know if that is a good or bad thing, but that is the way I grew up. You don't ever want to change if it is something you have always done and enjoyed and if it is something you want to continue doing.

When people hear your name, what do you think the first thing is that comes to their mind?

Crum: I don't know what comes to their mind, but what I hope comes to mind would be that we did it the right way. We did it playing the toughest schedules you could play every year and we had success doing it that way.

I never worried about the win-loss records so that enabled me to play tougher competition and better prepare ourselves. Our tournament record is very good, and I think the schedules that we played had a lot to do with that.

What don't outsiders know about Louisville that is so great?

Crum: Most of them don't know about the people, which make up the best and the worst of all communities. People here love basketball; they eat, live and sleep it. To be able to compete and satisfy them and be able to stay in one place for 30 years is rare, but those that are able to do that find that they are able to have a great quality of life.

During 30 years of coaching, how did you balance coaching and other things in life?

Crum: It just meant that you wouldn't get to do the other things you like as much and as often. But since I have been retired from coaching, I work here for the president at the university in the development office.

But I have a lot more time that I take for myself. I bought a place out in Idaho and I love fly fishing, and I spend six weeks out there each summer and I usually go to Alaska for five or six days of fishing each year. Last year I went to Chile, the year before I went to New Zealand and the year before that I was in Venezuela.

On Febrary 7, 2007, the floor inside Freedom Hall was renamed "Denny Crum Court".

Lute Olson
March 30, 2007

Atlanta traffic is bad. But it is even worse if you've driven 650 miles and are trying to stay awake after traveling through the night from northern Ohio. Taking more than an hour to travel the final 10 miles, we walked through the front entrance of the Hilton Hotel on Courtland Street NE at 8:30 a.m.

Despite the early hour, the enormous lobby was bustling with activity. Basketball people of all sorts were present, ranging from head coaches, to SIDs, to former players, to avid fans trying to sneak in a handshake or secure an autograph from a Final Four celebrity.

After milling around for what seemed like a long time, but was probably closer to 15 or 20 minutes, we found our way up the escalator to the second floor where the NABC (National Association of Basketball Coaches) was in a rules meeting.

One of the first people to leave the large gathering was Coach Olson, but before we had a chance to introduce ourselves, he disappeared around the corner. Caught in the stampede of the exiting coaches, we weren't sure what we were going to do and feared that we had very possibly missed our opportunity.

At that very moment my cell phone rang with an unknown number. I answered it and on the other end of the line was none other than Coach Olson himself, asking where we were and if we were ready to roll.

We walked in the direction that we had last seen him go and literally bumped into the veteran coach amid the madness and autograph seekers. Coach Olson led us to a relatively deserted corner on the second floor, near an opening that overlooked the ever-increasing chaos in the lobby below.

There were only two chairs in the vicinity. Obviously, Coach Olson occupied one and as the winner of the mental coin flip, Dave took the other, thus I took a knee on the opposite side of the long-time Arizona head coach.

Despite having talked with more than 20 coaches prior to meeting

In 1951-52, as a high school senior in Grand Forks, North Dakota, Coach Olson helped his team win the basketball state championship.

with Coach Olson, his interview was entirely unique. He went into great detail with regard to his player evaluation plan, a self-reflecting and peer ranking system that allows him to better open the lines of communication. It also provokes an open conversation with each player on where they stand and how they can improve both as an individual and as a teammate.

As we finished up following better than a half-hour conversation, Coach Few walked by and was asked in a joking manner by Coach Olson to "make yourself useful" and snap a picture for us.

As soon as the words left his mouth, another unidentified gentleman stepped forward and offered to take the shot, claiming to be a professional photographer.

We watched Coach Olson walk away and he quickly disappeared into a mass of people, much like the baseball players vanishing into the corn in the 1989 film, *Field of Dreams*.

From 1953-56, Coach Olson was a three sport athlete at Augsburg (Minnesota) College, starring in basketball, baseball and football.

On the second floor inside the Hilton Hotel
in Atlanta during the Final Four.

Lute Olson Profile

BORN:

September 22, 1934

HOMETOWN:

Mayville, North Dakota

HIGH SCHOOL:

Grand Forks - Grand Forks, North Dakota

COLLEGE:

Augsburg (Minn.) College - 1956

MAJOR:

Bachelor's: History and Physical Education

Coach Olson spent 11 seasons as a high school head coach and four as a junior college coach before acquiring the job at Long Beach State in 1973.

Lute Olson Year-by-Year

Year	School	W-L (Pct.)	Postseason
1973-74	Long Beach St.	24-2 (.923)	----
1974-75	Iowa	10-16 (.385)	----
1975-76	Iowa	19-10 (.655)	----
1976-77	Iowa	20-7 (.741)	----
1977-78	Iowa	12-15 (.444)	----
1978-79	Iowa	20-8 (.714)	NCAA (0-1)
1979-80	Iowa	23-10 (.697)	NCAA Final Four
1980-81	Iowa	21-7 (.750)	NCAA (0-1)
1981-82	Iowa	21-8 (.724)	NCAA (1-1)
1982-83	Iowa	22-9 (.710)	NCAA (2-1)
1983-84	Arizona	11-17 (.393)	----
1984-85	Arizona	21-10 (.677)	NCAA First Round
1985-86	Arizona	23-9 (.719)	NCAA First Round
1986-87	Arizona	18-12 (.600)	NCAA First Round
1987-88	Arizona	35-3 (.921)	NCAA Final Four
1988-89	Arizona	29-4 (.879)	NCAA Sweet Sixteen
1989-90	Arizona	25-7 (.781)	NCAA Second Round
1990-91	Arizona	28-7 (.800)	NCAA Sweet Sixteen
1991-92	Arizona	24-7 (.774)	NCAA First Round
1992-93	Arizona	24-4 (.857)	NCAA First Round
1993-94	Arizona	29-6 (.829)	NCAA Final Four
1994-95	Arizona	24-7 (.774)	NCAA First Round
1995-96	Arizona	27-6 (.818)	NCAA Sweet Sixteen
1996-97	Arizona	25-9 (.735)	NCAA Champions
1997-98	Arizona	30-5 (.857)	NCAA Elite Eight
1998-99	Arizona	22-7 (.759)	NCAA First Round
1999-00	Arizona	27-7 (.794)	NCAA Second Round
2000-01	Arizona	25-6 (.806)	NCAA Runner-Up
2001-02	Arizona	24-10 (.706)	NCAA Sweet Sixteen
2002-03	Arizona	28-4 (.875)	NCAA Elite Eight
2003-04	Arizona	20-10 (.667)	NCAA First Round
2004-05	Arizona	30-7 (.811)	NCAA Elite Eight
2005-06	Arizona	20-13 (.606)	NCAA Second Round
2006-07	Arizona	20-11 (.645)	NCAA First Round
34 Seasons		**781-280 (.736)**	

On March 29, 1983, Coach Olson took over the Wildcat program that the year prior was just 4-24. In his second season, the 'Cats won 21 games.

Interview with Lute Olson

What do you hope players take away from their experience with you?

Olson: One of the most critical things is that they continue to develop as a person in terms of their character, and they become more mature regarding what is expected of them.

I think that is one of the problems with the guys coming right out of high school and going into the pros. They make the mistakes in the pros that they really should have had the opportunity to learn through the discipline in the college situation, and would keep them out of the things that unfortunately happen in the pros. So I think it is the maturity and hopefully you can have an effect on character.

Having been part of basketball for almost 40 years what is the best advice you could give to a young coach?

Olson: Care enough about the kids to develop a personal relationship, so it is not just about basketball. Hardly ever when I get together with our guys do I talk about basketball. But I think if you care enough about them to develop a personal relationship, then I think you are going to accomplish a lot of things through that, that you are concerned about his feelings, concerned about his family life, and you are concerned about the things that he expresses to you he is concerned about. I think it is important that those lines of communications are opened immediately.

We have a sheet we have our players fill out three times a year to evaluate how they are doing in regard to the rest of the team. They evaluate on a spot between one through 13 who they think is number one, who is number two, things like who is the best hustler, who has the best team attitude, who has the poorest team attitude, etc.

I just do that to open the lines of communication, and I have a half an hour or 45-minute meeting with the kids after the evaluation is tabulated. They are tabulated with statistical methods where you eliminate the top two and bottom two scores so it is not a case of a person dinging somebody he doesn't like or somebody he is competing with. And mixing in the positives with the negatives, because what I really want to find out is if there is a problem attitude-wise with the kids, because the problem isn't going to get smaller but bigger, so it needs to be attacked immediately.

Enroute to the 1997 NCAA Championship, Arizona defeated three No. 1 seeds and three of the most prolific programs in history - Kansas, Kentucky and UNC.

That is why with a younger coach the biggest thing I try to get across is really try to show the kids that you are interested in them as a basketball player, and open the lines of communication to where I can sit with somebody that isn't realistic about where he is playing and I'll say, "Now that you are out of the mix, who would you put at number one? Who would you put at number two, three, four, and five all the way through 12?" Most kids are very realistic, but if a kid has himself at four and everyone else has him at nine, then you have a problem that is going to become a real serious problem.

So then what I do is ask the player, "You feel you are the fourth best player on the team, but your teammates feel you are eighth or ninth, and yet you have everyone else right on the money with what your teammates feel on the other spots." Then we get a chance to talk about it, what he feels he is doing for the team.

Little things like that in terms of communication, whatever a person can think of that would help you to get the kid to be realistic, and also recognize that, "Hey, we are on the same page." I want the same thing for you as you want for yourself, but how are we going to get to that?

The coaching part of it I think everyone understands. You need to teach fundamentals and your team is only going to be as good as your team fundamentals are.

But I think more importantly is developing the team attitude and team concept and getting the ego out of there and looking at it as "What can this person do by what he does to make the team better?" But when I talk to a young coach the first thing that I say is to open the lines of communication.

People typically retire in their mid-60's, but you being in your mid-70's and being responsible for motivating kids and boosters. How is it that you keep yourself motivated?

Olson: I have a passion for the game, and I have a passion for teaching. The basketball court is my classroom and I prepare for practices the same way I would prepare for class. I was a history major, and then I got my masters in guidance and counseling.

I try to look at it that same way, "Hey, I'm a teacher, not a coach!" But I love the game and I love the fact that I think you get closer to kids as a coach than anyone else. If you think about your playing experience in

DURING THE 1999-00 SEASON, COACH OLSON WON HIS 400TH GAME AT ARIZONA AND THE FLOOR INSIDE THE MCKALE CENTER WAS RENAMED "LUTE OLSON COURT".

high school, were you closer to the English or history teacher or with your basketball coach?

So I know the effects we have on kids. The interesting thing that I found is the tougher you have to be with somebody, the more he will probably resent that going through it, but once they leave your program, the further they get away, the more they appreciate it.

I think you can affect so many lives doing what I am doing and I know that if I weren't coaching I wouldn't have the opportunity to have the closeness with young people. Not only do I have a chance to change that kid's life, but how many people that person comes in contact with, like the ones that go onto coaching, how many kids they have affected.

That is why I continue doing it and I have always said I will coach as long as I have the energy and have the health. But I love what I'm doing. Am I frustrated at times? Very much so, but who isn't with a job? I think the important thing is that we understand that there are going to be good and bad things about everything, but I think for me the best thing I can do is coach young people and have an effect on their lives.

What was the original process in building the program at Arizona? When you took over, the Wildcats had just four wins the season prior.

Olson: My feeling is this, and it has always been this. If you start with good people, good people will find a way to be successful, but if you start with bad people, they are going to get you. They may not get you right now, but they will get you in the long run.

Bad people want to be with bad people, and good people want to be with good people. As soon as I got in at Arizona, we put a premium on the character of the kids we recruited. There are always problems when you come in. I have never been one to believe that you should just clean house when you first come in because I think you owe it to the kids that are there a little more than that.

The first year at Arizona I think we recruited seven kids, and all of them I thought were good people. Now some, like Steve Kerr, didn't have another scholarship offer but the character was there. Because of the good people we were able to get in the first group, in the next recruiting class we got really good people that might have been better basketball players.

But when we came to Arizona, you could walk in at halftime and

COACH OLSON WAS MARRIED TO HIS BELOVED WIFE ROBERTA "BOBBI" RUSSELL FOR 47 BEFORE HER PASSING IN 2001 AFTER BATTLING CANCER FOR NEARLY THREE YEARS.

take a front row seat, so the first thing we had to do was to market our program. A lot of coaches feel you don't want to bring on TV because then there are people watching out there that may have otherwise been at your game. I feel exactly the opposite in that if you are going to get those people to come to McKale you have to show them you have a good product, then they will come.

It is kind of like a restaurant that may be way the heck out of the way, but they build their clientele because they have a good product, and I really feel the same is true with basketball.

We have been sold out now for 20 years and one of the reasons I think we have been sold out is because our community sees our kids, student-athletes giving back to the community.

What have you personally taken away from coaching?

Olson: One, you have to be yourself, like I as a young coach went to clinics. I read every book Coach Wooden put out. I think it is important to research what you are doing to find out what the best things are, but then you have to be yourself in terms of teaching and coaching. There is no one that is going to show you a phony quicker than a kid.

I think I have made a lot of adjustments over the years as the kids have changed but down deep I don't think kids have changed that much. The surroundings have been so different - suddenly, if there are two parents both of them are working, and in most cases it is probably one parent because of the divorce rate.

The discipline in the high schools isn't the same as it once was, but I think down deep the young man wants discipline and direction. That I think is probably the biggest thing that I have gained from my experience is that recognition that kids are going to be different. In the end they all want the same thing, they want the ring. You will see it in the pros where guys will give up huge contracts to go to a team because they think they have a chance to win a ring.

I don't think you stay in the business as long as I have unless you are willing to adjust. Your thinking can change, but not the core values, they have to remain.

Following Bobbi's passing, Coach Olson requested the name on the floor in the McKale Center changed. Today it reads "Lute and Bobbi Olson Court".

John Chaney
March 31, 2007

We were instructed to have the front desk call Coach Chaney's Atlanta Hilton hotel room at 10 a.m. and go from there on Saturday morning. After several rings, he answered and asked if we could talk around 1 p.m. as he had been out late with friends and former colleagues.

With three hours of unexpected free time before our interview with the Temple legend, we mainly floated around the hopping hotel and saw a slew of recognizable faces.

The most notable person that we witnessed - other than the constant flow of big-time coaches - was former Cleveland Cavalier and Georgia Tech Yellow Jacket star Mark Price. A four-time NBA All-Star, and the all-time leading free throw shooter in NBA history, made his way through the crowd dressed in a suit and tie and quickly disappeared into an adjacent room.

At 12:45 we called Coach Chaney's room once more and shortly thereafter he met us at the front desk of the hotel, complete with a baseball cap and dark glasses amidst his blazer and unique shoes.

Before we could even finish introductions and greetings, several people noticed the 1988 Associated Press National Coach of the Year and a radio reporter actually sweet talked him into doing a brief radio spot, but only after Coach Chaney asked us if we had time and if it would be alright.

Remembering him on the Temple sidelines, he always gave the impression of a tough-nosed, no-nonsense, hardworking, blue-collar coach. We were told by several reputable sources that the Bethune-Cookman alum would be very honest, very open and very up-front with his responses.

While he was doing the radio interview, we staked out a quiet area near the back of the hotel and soon he returned. As we began the session, he seemed a bit guarded and his initial answers were short and to the point. However, after only a few minutes of feeling us out, the anticipated John Chaney persona began to come out in full effect.

A 1955 graduate of Bethune-Cookman in Daytona Beach, Florida, Coach Chaney was an NAIA All-American and a two-time all-conference performer.

He began to tell us the back stories to his responses and became very animated and passionate about a number of topics close to his heart. They included things such as education, family, making the most of yourself and how much more could be done with basketball to help improve the lives of the younger generations in this country that come from underprivileged environments.

At one point, he even apologized for his level of intensity as he spoke about the power of education in a person's life, and how one success story can lead and encourage others to pursue their aspirations.

We could have sat there for hours with Coach Chaney. He was a dynamic speaker that captivated our attention yet also let us converse. We didn't get the feeling that it was a one-way street with him doing all of the talking. His love for the game and more so for his players and friends really rose to the top during the 35 minutes that we sat with him.

Following his departure, we spent the afternoon at Hoop City, located inside the Georgia Libary of Congress. Filled with interactive booths, games and attractions, it was all the way around about basketball.

We listened to ticket prices to the semifinals on the street and were shocked to see thousands of dollars in cash being exchanged amongst strangers.

At the Hilton is where we wound up watching the games. In the lobby, there were big screen televisions everywhere. We pulled up lounge chairs, ordered some food and had a great time as about a dozen other fans joined us.

In 1978, Coach Chaney and Cheyney State in Pennsylvania won the Division II National Championship over UW-Green Bay, 47-40.

A somewhat quiet area on the first floor of the Hilton Hotel during the Final Four in Atlanta.

John Chaney Profile

BORN:

January 21, 1932

HOMETOWN:

Jacksonville, Florida

HIGH SCHOOL:

Benjamin Franklin - Philadelphia, Pennsylvania

COLLEGE:

Bethune-Cookman College - 1955

Antioch College - 1974

MAJOR:

Bachelor's: Physical Education

Master's: Education

On February 8, 1988, Temple earned the ranking of No. 1 in the nation for the first time in school history and finished the year 32-2, the best in school history.

John Chaney Year-by-Year (Division I only)

Year	School	W-L (Pct.)	Postseason
1982-83	Temple	14-15 (.482)	----
1983-84	Temple	26-5 (.806)	NCAA (1-1)
1984-85	Temple	25-6 (.833)	NCAA Second Round
1985-86	Temple	25-6 (.806)	NCAA Second Round
1986-87	Temple	32-4 (.889)	NCAA Second Round
1987-88	Temple	32-2 (.941)	NCAA Elite Eight
1988-89	Temple	18-12 (.600)	NIT
1989-90	Temple	20-11 (.645)	NCAA First Round
1990-91	Temple	24-10 (.706)	NCAA Elite Eight
1991-92	Temple	17-13 (.567)	NCAA First Round
1992-93	Temple	20-13 (.606)	NCAA Elite Eight
1993-94	Temple	23-8 (.742)	NCAA Second Round
1994-95	Temple	19-11 (.633)	NCAA First Round
1995-96	Temple	20-13 (.606)	NCAA Second Round
1996-97	Temple	20-11 (.645)	NCAA Second Round
1997-98	Temple	21-9 (.700)	NCAA First Round
1998-99	Temple	24-11 (.686)	NCAA Elite Eight
1999-00	Temple	27-6 (.818)	NCAA Second Round
2000-01	Temple	24-13 (.686)	NCAA Elite Eight
2001-02	Temple	19-15 (.559)	NIT
2002-03	Temple	18-16 (.529)	NIT
2003-04	Temple	15-14 (.517)	NIT
2004-05	Temple	16-14 (.533)	NIT
2005-06	Temple	17-15 (.531)	NIT
24 Seasons		**516-253 (.671)**	

Following the magical season in 1987-88, Coach Chaney was named the National Coach of the Year by the AP, NABC and numerous other outlets.

Interview with John Chaney

What do you hope players took away from their experience with you?

Chaney: I think that one of the most important things that players can ultimately feel good about is that they were in a structured situation. They have been in a situation where discipline is another higher form of intelligence. Also, to be able to say no to certain things, to be able to take inventory of your life, take inventory of things you do on a daily basis and be able to correct them and the mistakes that you make.

When most coaches use the word discipline, people think it is punishment, when really it is more organization, more structure and it is direction. My guys often talk about the kind of rules, thumb rules that I set for them. If you ever talk to them they will tell you there were always rules, there were more "don'ts" than "do's".

In fact, one time when my momma called, I thought my name was don't. There are more "don'ts" in your life than there are "do's" and I think those are some of the things my players took away.

What is the best piece of advice you could give to a young coach?

Chaney: He has to find a start in terms of being well-grounded, knowing that you are going to be working with the minds of young people. You are trying to right some wrongs in their lives, especially in the area of sports where success is spelled out in many ways with talent.

Often it is the will that overcomes everything, your will to accomplish, your will to do the right things. I think coaches have to be able to teach and instill that in many players, because you are going to be met with a lot of disappointments... it is not all winning.

In fact, there are some sports where you can go into the Hall of Fame failing. You can be successful in golf, it depends on the state of mind that you have. Nobody is ever going to play 18 holes and come away with a score of 18. In baseball, if you bat .300 you probably are going to the Hall of Fame, but you failed seven out of 10 times! It is something you have to deal with teaching youngsters to come to grips with, and I think coaches have to spell that out somewhere, and then think about serving.

Serving in the community, starting to work with community groups and serving in schools. But try to come up with some kind of service areas that you are going to be dealing with youngsters. You just can't

Coach Chaney led the Owls to five NCAA Elite Eight appearances, coming in 1988, 1991, 1993, 1999 and 2001.

hopelessly go into it without knowing how tough it is going to be in serving youngsters.

Was DI always your goal? When did you know coaching was for you?

Chaney: I didn't. That is the amazing thing. When I started in junior high school at a time when coaches didn't get paid, I was coaching baseball, gymnastics and basketball. As a physical education teacher, I was spending my evenings serving youngsters without any pay, so it was natural for me.

Then they started paying us and then the English teachers and math teachers came out of the dark and wanted to start coaching. I had no aspirations but there is always someone in your life that is a turning point whether it is a parent, some strong man, some strong woman that is in a leadership position that suggests we would like to see you here and that is what happened with me.

There was always a man who reached out and saw my worth and brought me along. And there was always someone who impressed me in that manner (As a player – Sam Brown, as a high school coach - Marcus Foster, in Division II coaching - Dr. Wade Wilson, Division I coaching - Peter Liacouras). I think that is what is lacking today in so many of our youngsters. There is no strong person that says this is what you are going to do, here are your "do's" and "don'ts".

What were the differences in coaching at each level?

Chaney: I still have a letter from Marcus Foster when he learned that I might leave Cheyney and go to Temple. You know how you are going from the known to the unknown, and you just don't feel good about it?

I was very apprehensive, I mean I was settled, and I just won a national championship in '78, went back to the Final Four and had another opportunity to win a championship at the Division II level. I was happy. I was a professor, I just won the teacher of the year award in the state of Pennsylvania. I was happy. Then all of a sudden someone came along and despite all of that wanted me to go to Temple.

I said, "Oh God, do I really want to go there?" But Marcus Foster wrote me a letter and said, "I want you to go to Temple because you are going to find that you can do more at that high level. Each level you go to, you will be able to do more." You just can't say no to some people.

Nine Atlantic 10 Players of the Year, seven regular season A-10 titles, six tourney titles and 296 conference wins were produced by Coach Chaney.

What does it mean to you to have a spot in the Hall of Fame?

Chaney: Well, that is the biggest thing when you are recognized by your peers, and that to me was the crowning of just about everything that I have done. And it does, once again, allow you to take inventory and reflect upon the reasons why you are here.

All of it took place as a result of so many people that were involved in my life, and you can't help but think about all of those men and my momma that were responsible for me getting there.

So when they only give you five minutes, Bill Walton called me up and said, "How do you get up there and talk about your life and talk about the people that are responsible for you being there without mentioning everybody you can think of? You just didn't get there by yourself!"

You get one moment in your life and at that one moment you can't imagine how you build up inside when you are trying to express what all of this really means... because it is more than the bouncing of a ball.

Thinking back over your career what are some of the most prominent memories that come to mind?

Chaney: I learned a long time ago that many of the youngsters, 85 percent of the kids I had, came from dysfunctional families - that is one-parent families or less.

What I honestly believe is that if you can get youngsters to believe in education and make education more affordable and accessible, we can get kids to change their lives around by simply going into a poor family where nobody has ever been to college, has never gone through or finished school.

Just take one kid from that poor family and take him through high school and college, then you could change the aspirations of every youngster thereafter as far as the neighborhood and family is concerned. That is the strongest thing I could suggest.

COACH CHANEY WAS INDUCTED INTO THE NAISMITH HALL OF FAME IN SPRINGFIELD, MASS. ON OCTOBER 5, 2001.

How do you feel about the current state of college basketball?

Chaney: I would like to see them do more. I spoke this morning to some of the guardians about the billions of dollars we bring, and I would like them do more about changing the culture in our school system.

I have had the chance to travel all around the world - Argentina, Japan, just about any place you can think of - and I have watched the school system in Japan. In Philadelphia we had about 300 killings last year and we are trying to change that culture of violence around.

You go into the criminal justice system and there are 500 kids in there that they are telling, "We will expunge your case in two years if you are a good person." Then, they go back out on the street and they come back, they are in the criminal justice system forever, all of their lives, so they are repeaters and they continue to repeat.

The only way you can change that is if you start at the early level, so we are getting together with Bill Cosby, Bon Jovi, Billy Cunningham, Sister Mary Scullion, Jim Bakker, and many others, and seeing if we can set up a Pilot program at the early levels for kids.

People do not understand that there are pockets of poverty where the gangs influence the kids more than families. There used to be a time where if a kid did something wrong, it would be embarrassing to him if he hurt his family. He wouldn't get in trouble because, "Hey man, I don't want my momma to find out, I don't want my papa to find out."

When I was sent home and was told to bring my mom back into school, she said, "I'm not missing work. You take your a-- back in there, I'm going to tell the teacher to kick your a--. You are just not going to make me lose my job by taking me into school."

Well, they empowered the schools, and that no longer exists. We want to change that dynamic by setting up a Pilot Academy of kids that go to school six days a week. See, you've got 40 percent of kids in Philly going to school, 60 percent of them don't go to school anymore, so if you are going to change that you can't change it at the upper level because high schools have turned into jails in these big city areas, believe me, jails.

If you are going to change that, you have to change it at the early level. My mother used to tell me, "If there is a lot of dirt underneath the rug, there is dirt on top of the rug, and if there is dirt on top, there is dirt underneath."

The dunk was illegal and then brought back in 1976, paving the way for Hakeem Olajuwon and Clyde Drexler's "Phi Slamma Jamma" teams at Houston in the early '80s.

Gene Keady
April 13, 2007

There is no quick way to get from Oak Harbor, Ohio, to Lafayette, Indiana. Instead of interstates and turnpikes, you have to take two-lane roads and surface streets that pass through small towns and farming communities. Yet the four-hour drive proved to be well worth it after Coach Keady guided us in and met us at the top of his twisting driveway.

Entering through the garage, we walked into the kitchen, past his office and were each offered a seat in the living room. In one corner sat the huge Naismith Award for his lifelong dedication to the game of basketball, which was awarded to him by the Naismith International Basketball Foundation in 2005. It was huge to say the least.

Our visit came just days after Coach Keady had been selected for the 2007 Wooden Legends of Coaching Award. The hardware was still enroute to his home as it was too heavy to transport by himself on the return flight from California where he accepted the honor.

Informing us that we were the first strangers that he had ever invited into his home, he also let us know that his wife was in the back bedroom with a .38 revolver under her pillow just in case. We think he was kidding, but we weren't completely certain at that moment.

Remembering his intimidating demeanor on the sidelines, Coach Keady was the exact opposite, nothing short of extremely kind for the entire two-hour conversation.

He started by recalling his days as a high school teacher in the state of Kansas and finished by chatting about his four months living in a hotel in Toronto while serving as an assistant coach for the NBA's Raptors.

Following the sit-down portion of the interview, Coach Keady showed us numerous souvenirs and mementos from his career. There were a lot more awards than space on the shelves and you could tell that while his awards are valued, he got much greater satisfaction from coaching and teaching young men than he did winning honors.

One of his favorite pictures includes one of the best from each level - high school legend Morgan Wootten, the "Wizard of Westwood" John

Wooden and the late, great builder of the Boston Celtics dynasty, Red Auerbach.

Maybe the coolest piece of history in Coach Keady's office was not a picture or a trophy, but an old baseball. In 1984, the Boilermakers were picked at the bottom of the Big 10 in the preseason voting. The athletic director at the time made a deal with Keady that if they were to win the conference, the baseball would change hands.

In league play, Purdue went 15-3 to capture the regular season championship. Not forgetting the wager, Keady collected on the bet and the baseball sits to this day on the shelf in his office. Its significance? It was autographed by none other than one of the greatest and most legendary players in baseball history, George Herman "Babe" Ruth!

Before leaving, Coach Keady provided both of us with a signed copy of his book - *The Truth and Nothing but the Truth.* We each snapped a picture with the retired Boilermaker and headed for home as he got set to watch the Raptors' game on television. At the time, they were making a push for the Atlantic Division title, which they would eventually win.

Coach Keady is a member of the National Junior College Hall of Fame, both as a player and as a coach.

Inside Coach Keady's home in West Lafayette.

Gene Keady Profile

BORN:

May 21, 1936

HOMETOWN:

Larned, Kansas

HIGH SCHOOL:

Larned

COLLEGE:

Kansas State University - 1958

Kansas State University - 1964

MAJOR:

Bachelor's: Biological Sciences and Physical Education

Master's: Education

As an assistant coach at Arkansas from 1975-78, Coach Keady helped the Razorbacks to a four-year record of 94-24 and the 1978 NCAA Final Four.

Gene Keady Year-by-Year (Division I only)

Year	School	W-L (Pct.)	Postseason
1978-79	W. Kentucky	17-11 (.607)	----
1979-80	W. Kentucky	21-8 (.724)	NCAA (0-1)
1980-81	Purdue	21-11 (.656)	NIT
1981-82	Purdue	18-14 (.565)	NIT
1982-83	Purdue	21-9 (.700)	NCAA (1-1)
1983-84	Purdue	22-7 (.759)	NCAA (0-1)
1984-85	Purdue	20-9 (.690)	NCAA First Round
1985-86	Purdue	22-10 (.688)	NCAA First Round
1986-87	Purdue	25-5 (.833)	NCAA Second Round
1987-88	Purdue	29-4 (.879)	NCAA Sweet Sixteen
1988-89	Purdue	15-16 (.484)	----
1989-90	Purdue	22-8 (.733)	NCAA Second Round
1990-91	Purdue	17-12 (.586)	NCAA First Round
1991-92	Purdue	18-15 (.545)	NIT
1992-93	Purdue	18-10 (.642)	NCAA First Round
1993-94	Purdue	29-5 (.853)	NCAA Elite Eight
1994-95	Purdue	25-7 (.781)	NCAA Second Round
1995-96	Purdue	26-6 (.813)	NCAA Second Round
1996-97	Purdue	18-12 (.600)	NCAA Second Round
1997-98	Purdue	28-8 (.778)	NCAA Sweet Sixteen
1998-99	Purdue	21-13 (.618)	NCAA Sweet Sixteen
1999-00	Purdue	24-10 (.706)	NCAA Elite Eight
2000-01	Purdue	17-15 (.531)	NIT
2001-02	Purdue	13-18 (.419)	----
2002-03	Purdue	19-11 (.633)	NCAA Second Round
2003-04	Purdue	17-14 (.586)	NIT
2004-05	Purdue	7-21 (.250)	----
27 Seasons		**550-289 (.656)**	

On April 11, 1980, Coach Keady was named the 17th men's basketball head coach in the history of Purdue University in West Lafayette, Indiana.

Interview with Gene Keady

What do you hope that your players took away from their experience with you?

Keady: Well, I hope they took away the discipline we taught them and took that discipline and put in their life where they can learn how to manage time, learn how to be competitive and learn how to get through discouraging moments by having strong character.

Then when you have a problem you have got to have faith and have families help you, and not think you can solve it all by yourself.

I just hope we taught our guys to be organized, and work hard, and treat people right, and have a good attitude about life, and enjoy each day the way you should enjoy it. If I did that to my players, I think I was pretty successful as a coach.

What would be the best advice you could give to a young coach?

Keady: Go see different people. It is a matter of seeing how different systems work, how different drills work, how you organize all of your different time elements.

It is really important to be a teacher and not a coach, especially to teach and not have people think, "Well I don't want to teach, I want to coach." Well, if you don't want to teach you are not going to be a coach. When I started in high school, I had to teach and that was good for me.

A little more common when you were in school, but to play four sports at Garden City Junior College, and then three sports at Kansas State. How were you able to do it?

Keady: I don't know, I organized my time, I just did it. If you love something, you find a way to do it, but you have got to understand in Kansas, in the 50s, there was not anything else to do. There were no computers, no games to play on your TV sets, so it was the best thing to do to stay out of trouble.

Would you say basketball was your favorite sport growing up?

Keady: Kansas basketball is kind of like Indiana basketball... it is king. It just kind of gets in your blood in Kansas, you are always shooting hoops in the winter, you are always playing hoops on the side of the

Coach Keady was named National Coach of the Year by numerous outlets after six different seasons - '84, '88, '94, '95, '96 and '00.

barn or in a hay loft. You are always doing something to stay out of the winter and play a game. It was just something that was part of my upbringing.

When I was an eighth grader, the high school where I lived won the state title, and that was huge. One of the senior guys on that team - and in those days you didn't idolize college students or pros because you didn't know them, but you knew your local guys who were good athletes - so I idolized this senior. He took me under his wing, and worked with me over the summer, and encouraged me to really study hard. I asked if I could get a scholarship someday, and he said, "Yeah, anybody can if you work hard, study hard, take care of yourself, have a good attitude, listen to your coaches and get better as a player."

I always tell that story because you don't know whose life you are touching as an older athlete, and you want to influence younger kids right, so he influenced me to go into college.

In 1989, you were up for the Arizona State job and we read that you walked into the Office of the President at Purdue, looked around and said, "I thought this was a once in a lifetime opportunity and I still do." What did you see that made you want to stay a Boilermaker?

Keady: I was in the President's office and I looked out over the campus, and I liked the bricks of the buildings - it was unified like a college campus should be. We were comfortable, we did well here, we had won three Big Ten championships at that time, and we liked everybody here.

Athletics at Purdue University is the only show in town. In the winter it is conducive to watching basketball, where at Arizona you can play baseball all year, or run track all year, or go outside and play golf all year.

But you know what the key was to why we didn't go? We had three dogs, and my wife and I were sitting there Sunday morning at ASU, and they flew us back on a jet that night. We kind of hoped that we (Purdue) were going to get into the NIT, but probably because of our losing record we weren't going to, but we came home early anyway.

So we came back, and we were lying there in our bed on Sunday morning and she said, "You know, it is really nice out there, we've done a pretty good job here, but it is awfully hot for our dogs." And I said, "What? If you are worried about our dogs getting overheated, that's it, we are not going."

In 1994, Glenn "Big Dog" Robinson averaged 30.3 points and was the consensus National Player of the Year. He was the No. 1 pick in the '94 NBA Draft.

What was your goal in writing a book - *The Truth and Nothing but the Truth* **- and your overall experience with that?**

Keady: When I was kid I read a lot of books that encouraged me to not give up your dreams. I wrote this book trying to get young people to understand that no matter where you start, never give up on your dreams. I grew up in a very poor family, my dad was a florist and made a dollar an hour and my mom worked at a 5 & 10 cent store.

I got a scholarship, went to college, got my degree, which was pretty big in our family. Then I became a high school coach. Then from a high school coach to a Big Ten team is hard to do, so don't give up your dreams. That is why I wrote my book, to tell kids to stay on course and keep your goals high.

With all these awards around here, which award has been the most meaningful to you or what memory stands out the most?

Keady: Probably the Abe Saperstein (founder of the Harlem Globetrotters) Award because the Globetrotters were part of my life growing up. How entertaining they were, and how much they encouraged young kids to keep their dreams alive and how much everyone enjoyed watching them play because they were showmen.

My phone ring is "Sweet Georgia Brown" (Harlem Globetrotters theme song), so that one probably means more than anything, but all of them do. I have some National Coach of the Year trophies in there that are very much cherished, and then the Naismith Award is huge. The grandson of Mr. Naismith gave it to me, and I don't know why they chose me, but they did.

Is there a story that the general public doesn't know about, just a good basketball story that you feel should be told more?

Keady: I was at Arkansas and went to the Final Four in '78, and really had a good team, and then I got the job at Western Kentucky.

So I go to Western Kentucky, and we did a good job our first year, and in the second year we won the league. Between the first and second year in '79, they used to have what they called sports festival teams - North, East, South, and West. They were college-aged kids, like sophomores and juniors that were potential Olympic hopefuls. It was an Olympic development thing, and we would get the 12 best players out of the East, 12

On seven occasions - '84, '88, '90, '94, '95, '96 and '00 - Coach Keady was named Big Ten Coach of the Year, tied for most in league history.

best players out of the North, 12 from the South, and 12 from the West, and we would go to Colorado Springs and practice for a few days. Then we would have games against each other, so you would play each team once, three games, then you would have the championship game.

I had the South, and I had James Worthy, Terry Fair, Jimmy Black, Darren Daye from UCLA - I don't know how he got in the South but he did - and Scott Hastings who played for us at Arkansas. We won the tournament by 25 points a game, nobody even came close to us.

And unbeknown to me, a guy who was on the Olympic committee by the name of Fred Schaus was the assistant A.D. (athletic director) here, and George King was the A.D. and my boss when I got here. In 1980 Lee Rose took Purdue to the Final Four with Joe Barry Carroll and he abruptly quit, like a week later he quit and he went to South Florida.

So Fred Schaus the previous year had watched me coach the South squad so when Coach Rose left here, Fred told George King, "The guy you need to hire is at Western Kentucky, young coach by the name of Gene Keady." And that is how I got the job here. He had watched me the previous summer at the Sports Festival and liked the way I coached and how the kids responded, and all of that. You never know who is watching you.

January 14, 2004 saw Coach Keady win his 500th game as the head coach at Purdue with a victory over Wisconsin, 53-51.

John Wooden
June 9, 2007

We never thought that we'd have the pleasure of meeting with Coach Wooden. Despite meeting so many other greats of the game, he remains on another level.

With some coaches we had to be very active and use multiple avenues in order to meet with them. They have a lot of help between secretaries, assistants and sports information directors. Coach Wooden has no one to help with his busy schedule except himself. Now well into his 90's, he lives alone in his Encino, California home where he has resided since 1972. Yet in doing a book on the greatest college basketball coaches we felt that one simple attempt would be fitting.

After Coach Crum spoke with Coach Wooden on our behalf, I called a number of days later and nearly couldn't speak when the "Wizard of Westwood" picked up the phone. We talked briefly and Coach Wooden asked me to call back after the Final Four when his schedule slowed slightly.

A week after Florida claimed their second straight title, this time in Atlanta, Georgia, I dialed Coach Wooden's number once more but got no answer. Former UCLA head coach Steve Lavin had advised me to leave my name and number on Coach Wooden's machine, so I did. Soon we learned that he had been admitted to the hospital, fortunately with a non-life threatening condition.

Several weeks later, around the end of April, I picked up my phone which I had vacated for no more than five minutes and found a new voicemail. It was from Coach Wooden.

In a state of shock, I dialed his number and within seconds we were chatting. He asked when a good time for us would be and I asked him when a good time for him would be. Eventually we settled on Saturday, June 9 at 10 a.m. at his longtime Encino home. I immediately called Dave and told him that whatever was going on from June 8-10 was now out - we were headed to meet the greatest of all-time!

On the afternoon of June 8, we flew into Los Angeles Internation-

At Martinsville H.S., Coach Wooden played on three teams that reached the state championship, losing as a sophomore and senior, winning as a junior.

al Airport and eventually checked into a hotel in Encino. Before heading to bed, we scoped out the area around Coach Wooden's place just to make sure there would be no problems in the morning.

By 8:30 a.m. we found ourselves at a local McDonald's within easy walking distance should the rental car had decided not to start.

At 9:30, the buildup and anticipation from five weeks of waiting really began to come to the surface. We were about to meet the best, the pinnacle, the man who every coach in the game looks up to and reveres.

The feelings that were going through us are impossible to describe. Coach Wooden is a human being just like everyone else, and he is a very humble individual, yet when you're talking about John Wooden, he is college basketball and so much more. A leader, a teacher and a man whose message has carried on strongly, despite being out of coaching for more than three decades. He is a legend and we were just a matter of feet from his door, poised with an invitation to enter.

At five until the top of the hour, I rang Coach Wooden's phone. He answered, said he would be right down, and immediately the large iron gate that leads to the underground parking garage began to slide open.

We spotted a nearby elevator and figured it was where he would appear. With time to assess the situation before the doors opened and despite being so close, we still could not believe that Coach Wooden was on his way down to greet us.

With a ding, the metal doors swung open and there he stood with the assistance of a wooden cane, dressed in a button down shirt, slacks and a UCLA-blue vest. We shook his hand and introduced ourselves as the doors closed behind us.

Before many additional words could be uttered, the elevator opened again. We stepped out and Coach Wooden pointed us toward the double-door entrance to his home. It isn't a huge place and by no means is it flashy in any sense of the word. It is filled to capacity with some of the greatest sports memorabilia anyone could ever imagine. Countless books line the shelves along with old photos and awards. In some places, memorable framed events line the floor - two, three, four-deep because Coach Wooden simply has no more room to hang them.

Once seated in the living room, we talked briefly about our project before delving into questions. He was remarkable. For over an hour we chatted about his career and his life. When his beloved late wife Nelly

COACH WOODEN WAS A THREE TIME ALL-AMERICAN - 1930, 1931 AND 1932 - WHILE A PLAYER FOR COACH WARD "PIGGY" LAMBERT AT PURDUE UNIVERSITY.

was mentioned, he even shed a tear. The two were married for 53 years until her passing in 1985.

As we concluded the interview, we thought that our time with him was concluding as well. Yet as he recited a poem as part of an answer to a final question, he asked if we'd like to hear more.

From there, he ushered us into his office, signed a number of autographs for us and then invited Dave and I to take his sportsmanship oath, which can only be done in his presence. We raised our right hands and repeated after him:

I'll be a good sport
When I win or I lose.
No whining, complaining, or making excuse.

I'll always keep trying,
One hundred percent
To give my best effort,
In every event.

This sportsmanship pledge
Will bring out my best.
Coach Wooden has taught me,
To be a Success.

He asked us to have a seat as he pulled out a book of poetry by one of his former players, Swen Nater. That second hour was even better than the first. After he finished several poems, which he probably could've read to us from memory, it was no longer an interview and we were no longer guests. We were conversing back and forth like old friends. He would ask us our thoughts on a particular topic and we would do the same.

More than likely, we could've stayed all day. But after two hours or so it was getting close to lunch time and we preferred to leave on our own before being asked. On our way out, Coach Wooden led the way and gave us the back-story on several pictures, including himself with Tiger Woods in one and President George W. Bush in another.

Escorting us to the door, we exchanged handshakes once more before

Leading the Boilermakers to the 1932 National Championship, Coach Wooden was nicknamed "The Indiana Rubber Man" for his reckless abandon on the court.

jumping back on the elevator. In the parking lot, we got a quick look at Coach Wooden's 1989 Ford Taurus, which he informed us has less than 40,000 miles of wear on it. By the time we got back out through the sliding metal gate, which wasn't much more than 30 seconds after entering the elevator, Coach Wooden had made his way through the entire house and was on the porch, standing next to his bucket of daily mail, waving goodbye to us as we returned to the car.

It truly was a once in a lifetime experience for us - that is the best way it can be described.

COACH WOODEN EXPERIENCED JUST ONE LOSING SEASON IN HIS CAREER AND IT CAME IN HIS FIRST YEAR AS THE HEAD COACH AT DAYTON HIGH SCHOOL IN KENTUCKY IN 1932.

The background is Coach Wooden's stone fireplace in the living room of his home in Encino, California.

John Wooden Profile

BORN:

October 14, 1910

HOMETOWN:

Martinsville, Indiana

HIGH SCHOOL:

Martinsville

COLLEGE:

Purdue University - 1932

Indiana State - 1947

MAJOR:

Bachelor's: English

Master's: Education

A lietenant in the U.S. Navy during WWII, Coach Wooden's appendix burst, keeping him from his first mission. His replacement was killed during an attack.

John Wooden Year-by-Year

Year	School	W-L (Pct.)	Postseason
1946-47	Indiana State	17-8 (.680)	----
1947-48	Indiana State	27-7 (.794)	NAIB Runner-Up
1948-49	UCLA	22-7 (.758)	----
1949-50	UCLA	24-7 (.774)	NCAA (0-2)
1950-51	UCLA	19-10 (.655)	----
1951-52	UCLA	19-12 (.613)	NCAA (0-2)
1952-53	UCLA	16-8 (.667)	----
1953-54	UCLA	18-7 (.720)	----
1954-55	UCLA	21-5 (.808)	----
1955-56	UCLA	22-6 (.786)	NCAA (1-1)
1956-57	UCLA	22-4 (.846)	----
1957-58	UCLA	16-10 (.615)	----
1958-59	UCLA	16-9 (.640)	----
1959-60	UCLA	14-12 (.538)	----
1960-61	UCLA	18-8 (.692)	----
1961-62	UCLA	18-11 (.621)	NCAA Final Four
1962-63	UCLA	20-9 (.690)	NCAA (0-2)
1963-64	UCLA	30-0 (1.000)	NCAA Champions
1964-65	UCLA	28-2 (.933)	NCAA Champions
1965-66	UCLA	18-8 (.692)	----
1966-67	UCLA	30-0 (1.000)	NCAA Champions
1967-68	UCLA	29-1 (.967)	NCAA Champions
1968-69	UCLA	29-1 (.967)	NCAA Champions
1969-70	UCLA	28-2 (.933)	NCAA Champions
1970-71	UCLA	29-1 (.967)	NCAA Champions
1971-72	UCLA	30-0 (1.000)	NCAA Champions
1972-73	UCLA	30-0 (1.000)	NCAA Champions
1973-74	UCLA	26-4 (.867)	NCAA Final Four
1974-75	UCLA	28-3 (.903)	NCAA Champions
29 Seasons		**664-162 (.804)**	

Deciding between UCLA and Minnesota, Coach Wooden accepted the job with the Bruins when the Golden Gophers didn't call back when they said they would.

Interview with John Wooden

What was the single greatest thing you hoped that your players took with them from their time with you?

Wooden: That they got a good college education that would be helpful to them all their life not just in sports, which will be just temporary.

How have your relationships been with past players over the years?

Wooden: Excellent. I have very close relationships. Almost every morning some of my ex-players will be at VIP's where we go for breakfast: Mike Warren, Andy Hill, Keith Erickson, Keith Wilkes, Lynn Shakelford, Andre McCarter, and on and on that I see quite regularly.

Bill Walton calls me three or four times a week, and comes up from San Diego with his wife about once a month and has breakfast at VIP's.

I know where most all the players that played for me in my 27 years at UCLA are. I know that there are close to 30 attorneys, eight ministers, several doctors, dentists, and teachers, businessmen and actors.

Two years ago at the McDonald's High School All American game back at South Bend, Indiana where I taught high school for nine years, they had a surprise luncheon for me. Twenty-some of my young men that had played for me at South Bend Central High School in the 30s were there. The oldest being 88 and the youngest about 80 along with several of their wives that I also had in English class. I have been in touch with many of them over the years. I have had a very close relationship with my ex-players.

What does it mean to you to have that close relationship?

Wooden: Well, they are extended family, and there is nothing more important than family. I taught English for years and years, and you did not get as close to your students in English class as you do in sports.

With sports you had them everyday; you had them not only under physical but also emotional and mental conditions, where in class it is generally mental and to some degree emotional, but you just get much closer to your athletes.

You grew up south of Indianapolis in Martinsville. When the Minnesota job came open when you were at Indiana State, you had offers from UCLA, and from Boston (Univ.) and Minnesota. At that time UCLA didn't have Pauley Pavilion or even an adequate practice gym. It is so different from Purdue and being a Midwest guy, and your Midwest friends and family were there. How did UCLA ever come up, and why did you consider it?

Wooden: I was offered the Purdue job but I was very displeased with the administration and the way they were treating the men I was replacing and told them I wouldn't work for them.

Then I was offered the UCLA and the Minnesota job, and I wanted to stay in the Big Ten. I did visit UCLA and many things I liked and many things I didn't like. I decided on those two, but Minnesota wanted me to keep the gentleman I was replacing as an assistant, and I didn't think that would be good for either one of us. I liked him very much, he had been the coach there when I played at Purdue, but I didn't think it would work because his philosophy of the game was a little different than mine. They had to find another position for him. They were to call me at a certain time, an hour before UCLA wanted a final answer.

Minnesota didn't call and UCLA called and I accepted, and an hour later Minnesota called and said, "Everything is okay!" But I said, "It's too late, I'm sorry, I have committed myself and I can't back out on a commitment."

I can't tell you exactly why I left Indiana State, I was happy there. I had all the players I had my first two years and we got better each year. I think we were 17-8 my first year, and 27-7 the second year, and I had them all back. It was home in Indiana, we had a baby and everything, but I just felt, my wife and I felt it might be good to make a change.

I had the visit out here, liked certain aspects, other aspects I didn't. But one of my dearest college friends was on the football coaching staff, and he thought that with UCLA I had a great future. It was going to be difficult, particularly for basketball, but he thought I had a great future. The first couple of years I wondered why in the world I ever did it.

At what point could you call Los Angeles home?

Wooden: Had I not signed for a three-year contract when I came - and I was the one who insisted on a three-year contract - I would have

Winning the conference title in 1947, Coach Wooden rejected an offer to play in the NAIB Tournament because Blacks were not allowed to participate.

left after two. But after three years, my children were getting pretty well settled and I was getting more settled and accepting of the situation for what it was.

Indiana is still home, it will always be home, I am a Hoosier. I would say in four or five years it felt comfortable in saying this felt more like home. There are so many things here that you don't realize from back at home.

For example, from where we sit, in an hour or two I could be on the ocean, in an hour or two I could be in the mountains, in an hour or two I could be in the desert, in an hour or two I could be at Disneyland, in an hour or two I could be at the zoo, in an hour or two I could be at a sporting event of professional or intercollegiate or interscholastic whatever is in season, in an hour or two I could be at a late play, so many things within an hour or two.

I have never had to use chains on my car. I don't have any heavy clothes at all, and I don't need an overcoat or overshoes. At times, there is the danger of an earthquake, but no danger of tornadoes which we had back in Indiana. I haven't been in a storm cellar out here. It grows on you.

Do you like all the traffic? No. Do you have to be in it? Not necessarily, you can work yourself around it. But wherever you are, there are pluses and minuses. And an American of whom I have the greatest respect is Abraham Lincoln, who once said, "You are going to be about as happy as you make up your mind to be, and the best place you can be is where you are."

When you were recruiting players, aside from talent, with you being so big on character, what was your approach to recruiting?

Wooden: I didn't believe in visiting homes, I visited very few homes. I never wanted to talk a player into coming, I wanted him to know what we had, and have them make their visit and know what we had, and then I wanted them to want to come. My idea was a little different from most, and maybe it wouldn't succeed today, but a lot of people didn't think it would succeed in my day either.

If I were recruiting you I'd say, "If you come here now, you understand to begin with you won't like it for a while, and in your first year you will be saying, "Well I should have gone some place else. But if you

A YEAR LATER, CLARENCE WALKER BECAME THE FIRST AFRICAN-AMERICAN TO PLAY IN THE TOURNAMENT AFTER THE NAIA CHANGED THEIR POLICY.

had gone there you would be saying the same thing because you are going to be away from home for the first time. You've left friends that you have grown up with. Academically you are going to be around a lot of outstanding students. So you will be unhappy, but if you are going to be unhappy, why not be unhappy with us for a year? You will get over it."

It became, and I think this is normal, success breeds success. I have been asked, "How come it took you fifteen years to win your first national championship?" And I responded, "Well, I'm a slow learner." But you notice that once I learned it, I had it down pretty well.

We won more conference championships than any other school in our conference by quite a margin, but we were getting eliminated rather quickly in the first or second round. Except in '62 when we went to the Final Four and lost to Cincinnati, who won the championship on a last second shot. Just the fact that we got to the Final Four, got us nationwide attention.

Two years later we won our first national championship and that attracted the attention of Lewis Alcindor, and he was a junior and he watched it on television with his coach, and he said, "That is one of the schools I want to visit next year."

The next year (1965) we repeated as national champions against Michigan and that sort of solidified his interest. Then he (Lew Alcindor) visited our campus, and Pauley Pavilion. I took him up to show it and told him, "You will be a player on the first team to play in the best place on the coast." Which it was at the time. But if we hadn't won that first championship we wouldn't have attracted his attention.

I never believed in, as I say, "trying to talk players". I wanted them to want to come. I wanted to know all about them. I'm a nut on quickness, in any sport. I think quickness under control, if it's not under control you have activity, but you don't have achievement, so I wanted quickness under control. That is what I was looking for in all athletes.

For example, I think my two great centers, they were big, but there were a lot of other big centers, but very few quicker than Alcindor and Walton. They were very quick, not great speed, not bad, but they were quick.

I was hoping my center would be quicker than my opposing center, guards quicker than other guards and forwards quicker than other forwards. I wanted three that were quicker than the opponents. You would

UCLA rattled off 88 wins in a row between 1971-1973, winning the seventh, eighth and ninth championships during Coach Wooden's tenure.

like to have all five of course, but I think that was asking for too much.

Obviously you talk to a lot of young coaches, what is the best piece of advice you give to a young coach?

Wooden: At the top of my pyramid, on the one side is patience and the other side is faith. You have to have patience, and you have to believe, you have to believe. You have to feel that things are going to work out as they should, providing that you do what you should to help make them become a reality. At times we get caught up in wanting things to happen and we don't do everything we are capable of doing to help that - we just want it to.

So I would say that when I talk to young coaches, have patience and realize at the beginning how little you know. I would say that the older you get, in teaching or anything else, the older you get always remember how little you know. When you start you know less about it, but you should always be learning. If you are still learning it's good.

Is there anything in your life that you would go back and change?

Wooden: I would like to say in teaching there is not a thing I would change. I made a decision. I thought that decision was right, so I would not change it. I don't care how it worked out, that's it, just because it doesn't work out the way you hoped doesn't mean it is wrong. If I make a decision because the alumni thinks so, or the media thinks so, or somebody else thinks so, that is wrong. I have to make the decision based upon what I think, and that is the right decision.

As for my personal life if I could change, I would have tried to have done more for my late wife, and that would be the one thing. She loved to dance, and I didn't, I wouldn't go to dances, but she would go to games and things with me. But still we had a wonderful life, and that caused no friction, but when I look back if I had to change I would do more for her.

A lot of people know certainly from the books you wrote with Mr. Jamison and others, a lot of the big-time stories from UCLA, with Lew Alcindor and Bill Walton and his haircut. Is there a story that does not get told enough, or that is a lesser-known story that comes to mind that you could share with us?

In 1999, ESPN annointed Coach Wooden the "Greatest Coach of the 20th Century".

Wooden: Any number of my players that were academic All-Americans and practically all of my players, practically all of them graduated, got their degrees, and that is not paid much attention to - it's if they won championships. Why are they here in school? To win championship basketball tournaments? I don't think so. It's to get a good education, and I was very happy to see that practically every player I had graduated and all have done well or reasonably well in whatever profession they chose.

But I would say that what is not known is how many academic All-Americans I had, and I can't tell you the exact number myself, but we had an awful lot of them, and in fact practically every player graduated, and that is my greatest pride and satisfaction.

What is the question, or questions, that you get asked the most?

Wooden: The questions I really get asked the most, are "Which team that you had did you think was the best? Which player was the best?" I'd say more than anything else I am asked those questions.

If your father would ask me, "Which player was the best?" I would say, "Do you have any children? Which was the best?" Actually, it is not trying to evade the question, but how can you really say? You can't.

I can say that I never had a more valuable player than Lewis Alcindor, I can say that I never had a better all around player than Bill Walton. I can say I never had a smarter player than Mike Warren, a point guard. I can say I never had more spirited players than Keith Erickson, or Gale Goodrich, or David Meyers, but never will I say, "This was the best."

In 2003, Coach Wooden was at the White House to receive the "Presidential Medal of Freedom, the highest honor bestowed upon a civilian.

Ben Howland
June 9, 2007

Originally we were scheduled to meet with Coach Howland on Friday, just hours after deboarding our non-stop flight out of Detroit. Yet by the time we got our luggage at LAX and made it through the turnstiles of the rental car facility, we realized that the 405 freeway traffic was going to make it impossible for us to get to his office at the appointed time.

Leslie Dalziel, Coach Howland's secretary, said that she would try to get us a time later in the weekend and would call us back shortly. We felt fortunate that Coach Howland was willing to meet with us while we were in LA to talk to Coach Wooden, and to miss our scheduled appointment was extremely frustrating.

We were just a matter of miles from his office after traveling across the country but were unable to get there due to the infamous Los Angeles traffic.

Very soon, Leslie called back and informed us that she had arranged for us to meet with Coach Howland at 5:45 p.m. the following day in his office in the J.D. Morgan Center, located next door to Pauley Pavilion, the home of Bruin basketball.

On Saturday, after leaving Coach Wooden's home around noon, we had a few hours to spend and decided to check out Malibu, located not far west from UCLA along the coast.

You've probably heard a lot about the breath-taking sites in Malibu, and they are completely true. As we arrived from the north, the mountains gave way to the sea and on our right came into view a large, green hill, with Pepperdine University located at its peak, and dozens of deer grazing leisurely.

After turning east onto the Pacific Coast Highway, the mountains are located on the left with mansions and large estates built right into the side of the cliffs and on the right is the Pacific Ocean, allowing you to view the Southern California coast for miles on a clear day.

By 3:30 we parked the rental car in a UCLA parking garage and began walking around the beautiful campus, which features a vast amount of rolling hills and mountains looming in the distance. The campus was bustling with activity as finals week approached. We went inside the library and found scores of students finishing papers and hovering over their books and computers.

As we circled back to the J.D. Morgan Center we listened to the alumni band playing for a university fundraiser and sat on a bench near the entrance. Before long Coach Howland walked up to us, introduced himself and showed us to his second floor office.

While he grabbed a few things, we noticed the decorations in his office, which included several large framed items from Coach Wooden along with the 2006 national runner-up trophy and the 2007 regional championship trophy.

With a demeanor similar to that of his good friend and successor at Pittsburgh, Jamie Dixon, we jumped right into our line of questioning of the Bruins coach. From behind his large wooden desk, Coach Howland quietly answered our inquiries despite his needed presence at the already in-progress fundraiser.

Twenty-five minutes later, we wrapped things up with a picture and got Coach Howland on his way as we made our way back to the car. Considering ourselves lucky to have avoided a parking ticket, we spent the evening checking out some of the sites.

We drove past the famed Beverly Hills sign, up and down Rodeo Drive featuring some of the most upscale and expensive stores around. We ended up in a hotel in Burbank, not far from Alameda Avenue where the Tonight Show with Jay Leno is taped each weeknight.

It was more than $100 for the night, but don't let the price fool you, it was a hole! Passing the pile of burned out mattresses upon exiting in the morning, we felt dirty despite grabbing showers. Compared to our other travels, we really lived it up in California by flying out, driving a mid-level rental car, and staying in a hotel for two straight nights.

As a graduate assistant at Gonzaga in 1981-82, Coach Howland worked with the NBA's all-time assists leader John Stockton.

Coach Howland's office. Just out of view sit the trophies from UCLA's runs to the Final Four in 2006 and 2007.

Ben Howland Profile

BORN:

May 28, 1957

HOMETOWN:

Lebonon, Oregon

HIGH SCHOOL:

Cerritos - Cerritos, California

COLLEGE:

Weber State University - 1979

Gonzaga University - 1981

MAJOR:

Bachelor's: Physical Education

Master's: Administration and Physical Education

From 1982-1994, Coach Howland spent a dozen years as an assistant at UC-Santa Barbara.

Ben Howland Year-by-Year

Year	School	W-L (Pct.)	Postseason
1994-95	N. Arizona	9-17 (.346)	----
1995-96	N. Arizona	7-19 (.269)	----
1996-97	N. Arizona	21-7 (.750)	NIT
1997-98	N. Arizona	21-8 (.724)	NCAA First Round
1998-99	N. Arizona	21-8 (.724)	----
1999-00	Pittsburgh	13-15 (.464)	----
2000-01	Pittsburgh	19-14 (.576)	NIT
2001-02	Pittsburgh	29-6 (.829)	NCAA Sweet Sixteen
2002-03	Pittsburgh	28-5 (.848)	NCAA Sweet Sixteen
2003-04	UCLA	11-17 (.393)	----
2004-05	UCLA	18-11 (.621)	NCAA First Round
2005-06	UCLA	32-7 (.821)	NCAA Runner-Up
2006-07	UCLA	30-6 (.833)	NCAA Final Four
13 Seasons		**259-140 (.649)**	

Coach Howland took Northern Arizona, a seven-win team in 1996, to three consecutive years of 21 wins before taking the reigns at Pittsburgh in 1999.

Interview with Ben Howland

What do you hope that players take away from their time with you?

Howland: First of all, I hope they had a really good experience playing, learning, and improving. The whole thing about being a player is to continue to develop and continue to improve throughout your career, whenever that may end.

But I also want my players to have had a fulfilling experience, where they have really enjoyed playing. Hopefully they have learned some things that carry over to real life through their opportunities of playing at a high level of basketball, because you do have a lot of correlation between things you learn as in goal setting, sacrifice, commitment to a team in whatever you are doing, being unselfish, and doing your very best everyday. All of those things carry over to the real world, of being disciplined, being focused, and being able to deal with adversity.

Obviously expectations at UCLA are always through the roof, how do you, your staff and your players deal with such high expectations?

Howland: Well we embrace them. I mean that is why you come to UCLA. I had a pretty good situation at Pitt, and we probably could have stayed there for a long time.

UCLA has the greatest tradition in all of college basketball, so therefore you want to, if you have the opportunity, to be in that situation. You obviously have high expectations that come with that, but I think that helps us actually because the players know that is the deal.

When we are at home people say, "There is nothing to do here, and we would like to be somewhere else." You can't find a place with more to do than LA, so when you are recruiting, do you have to recruit kids with even more character to deal with this environment?

Howland: A lot of the kids we are recruiting are from this area, so it is not a big change as far as environment that they are coming into.

Most of the guys we recruit have high expectations and goals for themselves as individuals, too. They are trying to get beyond the college level, so they are pretty focused on their career and being the best they can be. Yeah, they all want to have fun. There is a lot to do, and we expect them to have fun and have a good time. But in our situation, you

In his final two seasons at Pitt, Coach Howland put together a record of 57-11 overall, 32-1 at home and two NCAA Sweet Sixteen appearances.

are in a fishbowl. Everybody knows who these kids are, so it becomes a pretty big responsibility to be a player here.

Having just taken over a prominent program like UCLA, what is your mentality when coming into a new program?

Howland: It is really simple: surround yourself with really good people. I mean the quality of your staff and your assistant coaches is critical.

The number one thing with any program in terms of its success is getting good players. Then being able to recruit, and getting kids that fit the profile for whatever university you are at. With that said, you have to get really good players. I can be as good a coach as I want to be, but if you don't have the talent to work with it doesn't matter.

Now, there are coaches that have really good talent that don't have great success, but you never have a lot of success without really good players, and any coach will tell you that, it's that simple.

Others credit your teams for playing stiff, tight, man-to-man defense. How do you get a team to buy into playing that style of defense?

Howland: The best defensive teams typically win championships in whatever sport you are talking about, not just basketball. But in terms of getting teams to play good defense, number one is getting kids that are athletic, strong, and tough. It is also getting enough number of kids to where you can rotate guys when they are not doing their jobs.

Even when we have a bad night on offense, we can still have a chance to win the game if we are playing good defense, and that has been proven out over the last couple of years. Good defense has given us an opportunity to get pretty far in the past two tournaments, and hopefully we can finish one off here soon.

With UCLA comes John Wooden, what is your personal relationship with him, and when you think of him, is there a special experience that comes to mind?

Howland: You know with Coach, number one, this is his program, and I am just the current caretaker. I really feel fortunate to be the coach, because as a coach here you do get to have a relationship with John Wooden. The thing I marvel about him more than any other thing is

On April 3, 2003, Coach Howland was named the 17th coach in UCLA program history.

that, for as good a coach as he was - and he is the greatest coach in the history of basketball and probably all of sports, in any sport - he is even a better person. I am sure you got a sense of that today just with spending some time with him. Just how giving he is of himself for others, his whole life is about affecting other lives and helping others. He is a good Christian, he is a good man, he is a good father, he was a great husband, and he is a great role model for everybody.

Can you give us a little Coach Howland on Coach Howland - what aspects of coaching do you work extra hard to improve on?

Howland: I am always trying to improve different aspects of what we do. Although, I probably won't work on being a zone coach anytime soon, I don't believe in that. But being able to adjust, and you have to adjust to your talent, and adjust to your level of different players you may have year in and year out to a certain degree, but basic things we are going to stand by.

I am always looking to learn from others. Most of the plays or sets that we run aren't things that I have invented, but are things I've watched other people do and liked and tried to fit into what we do. I also hope I can be a better recruiter, and a better coach in all aspects. Offensively and defensively we also try to get better.

I'm also open to new ideas. I just lost another assistant, so that is three coaches now that have left in the last two years to go onto head coaching jobs. So that is always helpful to get some ideas from the new coaches that come in.

Coach Howland has been a conference coach of the year in three different leagues - Pac-10, Big East, Big Sky - in just 13 seasons as the lead man.

Coast-to-Coast...

Destination Basketball involves coaches from 18 states. Those states border the Atlantic Ocean, the Pacific Ocean, the Gulf of Mexico, the Great Lakes, Canada and Mexico.

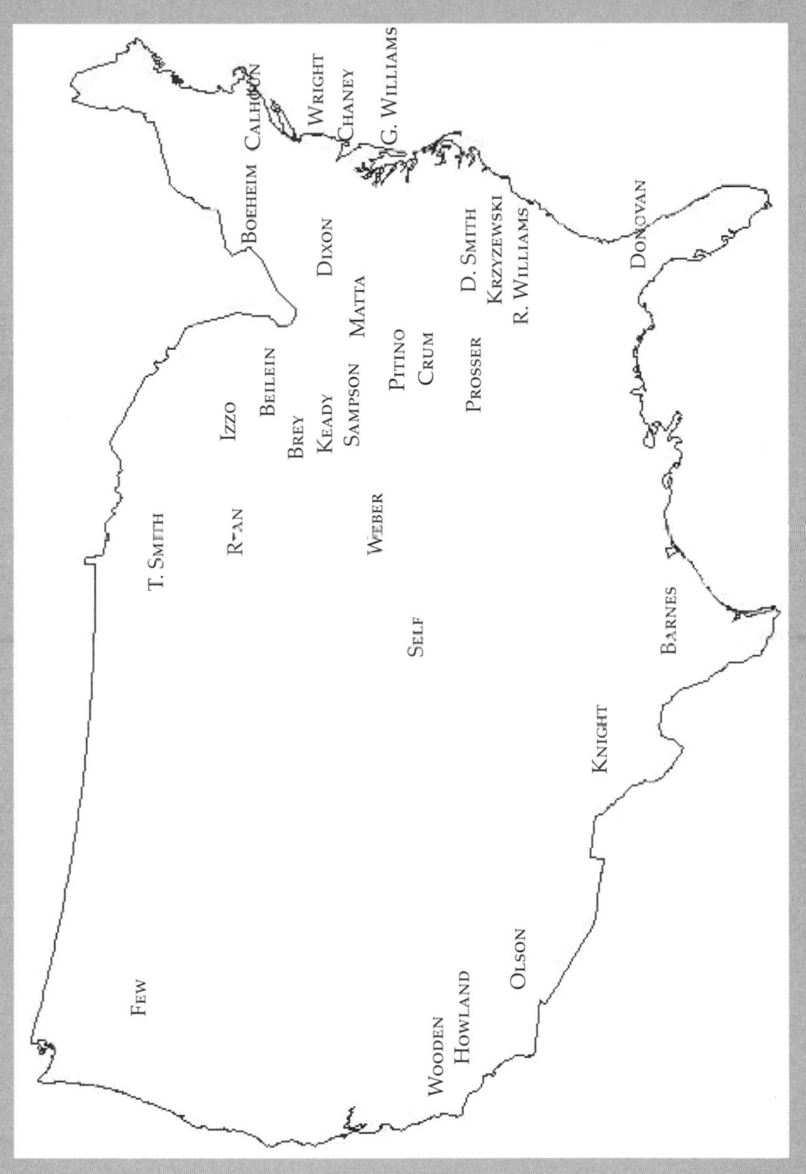

In the history of the tournament - dating back to 1985 - no 16-seed has ever defeated a top ranked squad. However, a number of two-seeds have fallen.

Billy Donovan
August 1, 2007

Our first trip to Gainesville, Florida, came on July 24, 2006, hours after meeting with Dick Vitale for breakfast on Siesta Key near Sarasota. The Gators had won their first national championship approximately four months earlier, crushing UCLA, 73-57.

Flash forward one year, one week and one day - our second experience in the land of the Gators - and this one included face time with UF head coach Billy Donovan, the now two-time national championship winning coach.

Honestly, it took us 373 days to land an interview with him, which when you think about it is a great sign for the state of college basketball. It would not be good if he were relatively non-busy and his time was easily accessible.

Before departing home at 3 p.m. on July 31, someone asked us how to get to Gainesville from Oak Harbor, Ohio, and it really is pretty simple. You take Ohio State Route 105 to Interstate 75 South, drive for nearly 1,000 miles through five states, get off at Exit 387, turn right and you'll run right into the University of Florida.

That's exactly what we did and after driving straight through, we arrived on campus at 6:30 a.m. Completely exhausted following the 994-mile excursion, it was disheartening to witness dozens of UF student-athletes running during the early hour as we battled to keep our eyes opened and focused.

Our appointment, set up through Florida SID Fred Demarest, was originally scheduled for 1 p.m. However, we let him know before leaving that we would arrive early in case a change in Coach Donovan's schedule occurred. He also had gone through a long evening the night prior, recruiting up North before flying home.

We got Fred on the phone at about 7:15 as we laid back in our seats in the car and he said that he would contact us immediately if Coach Donovan would be available earlier. Basically, if we didn't have to wait until the afternoon we could be back in northern Ohio at a somewhat

Playing for Coach Pitino at Providence as a senior in 1987, Coach Donovan averaged 20.6 points and led the Friars to the NCAA Final Four.

reasonable hour. The drive, without traffic problems, eats up about 15 hours each way.

Following a nearly hour-long nap in the already hot, humid and sun-drenched car, Fred called us and said that Coach Donovan would be ready for us in less than five minutes. Still dressed in shorts and t-shirts, and looking pretty ragged, the call provided a much needed adrenalin boost and propelled us into action much like a fire drill.

Undressing and redressing in the very visible parking lot across from the basketball practice facility, we ran through our checklist of necessary items for the interview - recorder, camera, list of questions - and ran to meet Fred at the front entrance.

Following him up the twisting stairs, we entered the offices on the second floor and walked by the assistants' space before popping our heads into Coach Donovan's hardwood-floored office, located at the end of the hall on one corner of the building. Fred introduced us and exited as we shook hands with Coach Donovan and took a seat in front of his desk.

For whatever reason, I think we anticipated his personality to be similar to that of a cold, calculating businessperson with his short, slicked-back hairstyle, piercing stare and New York roots. We didn't expect him to be overly friendly but he was, very much so. It was somewhat similar to our time with Coach Pitino. We didn't expect either to provide anywhere near the level of warmth and invitation that they did.

Coach Donovan went so far as to offer us his help within the college hoops world. And we took it as a very genuine offer. Sometimes people say "stay in touch" or "let me know how I can help" and you know that they're just being nice. We left our 20-minute session with Coach Donovan very excited and happy to know that a guy who is at the top of his profession, and who is busier than you could ever believe, would offer us a little bit more of his most precious resource and asset, his time.

THE 5-11, 170-POUND GUARD WAS DRAFTED BY THE UTAH JAZZ IN THE 3RD ROUND AND PLAYED 44 GAMES WITH HIS HOMETOWN NEW YORK KNICKS IN 1988.

Inside Coach Donovan's office at 9 a.m. after driving all night from Ohio - nearly 1,000 miles.

Billy Donovan Profile

BORN:

May 30, 1965

HOMETOWN:

Rockville Centre, New York

HIGH SCHOOL:

St. Agnes - Long Island, New York

COLLEGE:

Providence College - 1987

MAJOR:

Bachelor's: General Social Studies

After playing a season for the Knicks in 1988, Coach Donovan spent some time on Wall Street working with an investment banking firm.

Billy Donovan Year-by-Year

Year	School	W-L (Pct.)	Postseason
1994-95	Marshall	18-9 (.667)	----
1995-96	Marshall	17-11 (.608)	----
1996-97	Florida	13-17 (.433)	----
1997-98	Florida	14-15 (.483)	NIT
1998-99	Florida	22-9 (.710)	NCAA Sweet Sixteen
1999-00	Florida	29-8 (.783)	NCAA Runner-Up
2000-01	Florida	24-7 (.744)	NCAA Second Round
2001-02	Florida	22-9 (.710)	NCAA First Round
2002-03	Florida	25-8 (.758)	NCAA First Round
2003-04	Florida	20-11 (.645)	NCAA First Round
2004-05	Florida	24-8 (.750)	NCAA Second Round
2005-06	Florida	33-6 (.846)	NCAA Champions
2006-07	Florida	35-5 (.875)	NCAA Champions
13 **Seasons**		**296-123 (.706)**	

In winning back-to-back National Championships,
the Gators broke 64 individual and team records.

Interview with Billy Donovan

What do you hope your players take away from their time with you?

Donovan: Well, I think the biggest thing that we would like to have happen here is for them to be prepared for life. For a lot of these guys that entails a lot of different things. Most of these kids come in and their first dream and goal is to play in the NBA, but you also realize that there are a lot of kids that are not talented enough play in the NBA.

Then, the next step is a lot of those guys would like to go overseas and play, so you would like to try have them as prepared as they can be to compete at that next level: compete professionally, be prepared professionally, and to know how to conduct themselves professionally.

Then I think the other part is that guys take their majors and put their focus on them over a four-year period here. We try to get them prepared for the workplace, about the importance of being on time, the importance of working hard, the importance of being part of a team, the importance of sacrificing. We have had guys get into a lot of different fields and do a lot of different things and you hope when they leave this program that they are prepared to understand what it is to work, to be responsible, sacrifice, and be part of a team.

You played for Coach Pitino, you coached with him, can you talk about the biggest lesson that you learned from him that has helped to shape you as a coach and as a person?

Donovan: The biggest thing is the work ethic piece of it. I think I am living proof that a 5-11 guard with limited athletic talent, through hard work, and perseverance, and dedication, can accomplish a lot.

I think the biggest thing I took from Coach Pitino is that if you have passion for something in life, and you love something, if you put your heart and soul into it, and you work at it, and you have that passion for the right reasons, a lot of great things can be accomplished.

I think he was probably the one guy that took my work ethic and my love for the game and I probably mirrored his work ethic and love for the game. He built up my self-esteem, made me really believe in myself, and then I had the chance to experience incredible things as a player and then obviously working for him.

On March 27, 1996, Coach Donovan began his tenure as the leader of the Gators at the ripe old age of 30.

Obviously it is special to be part of the NBA, what was your experience as a player in the league?

Donovan: To me a lot of times God is always looking over you, and for me growing up in New York, my dream was to always play for the Knicks and you realize that even though you dedicate yourself, you work hard, and give everything you have to the game, there are no guarantees of what is going to happen or how it is going to work out.

The thing that was amazing to me when you look back on it, is the timing of the way things happened from Coach Pitino coming into Providence College, to have the chance to have two incredible years, to get drafted, and then for him to pick up the phone and actually have him be the Knicks coach for that time.

To be able to go back and play for the Knicks, it really was a dream come true. Although it was a short-lived dream, it was an experience that I got a chance to put on an NBA uniform, not only an NBA uniform, but I got a chance to put on an NBA uniform where I grew up in New York.

I just don't think that happens without some divine intervention, and I think maybe playing the game for the right reasons, my love and passion for the game, I was blessed to be able to experience something like that. I would have loved to have had, as many players do, a long NBA career, but I got the chance to do the next best thing, which was coach.

Has it been more rewarding for you taking a non-traditional football school in basketball to greater success as opposed to a program like Kansas, Duke, or Kentucky where success is already expected?

Donovan: Someone made a great comment to me that it is very rare in life that you get the chance to start off with something at the ground floor and be part of the building process all the way up. The building process here was not only myself, it was the administration, the president, the athletic director, our coaches and the players, but I think we were able to do something that was totally against the norm.

If you really look at the "traditional football schools", I don't know how many of those schools have actually won basketball national championships, and have had the chance to win two of them.

Coming in here I really embraced the whole football situation. I think the football situation here is great for us, it shows the passion and the

He is the winningest coach in Florida history with 261 victories in 11 seasons, an average of 23.7 triumphs per season.

energy for this university, and I also think there is a strong commitment fan support-wise for basketball. The greatest overriding factor here is that people here support the University of Florida, love the University of Florida more than anything else... there is a great pride here.

You don't win 35 games each year, and you certainly can't win a national championship every year. How do you keep everyone at bay, especially big Florida fans, but not necessarily big basketball fans?

Donovan: I think that's the nature of the beast right now with the internet and talk radio, and people being able to express opinions more openly out there. It has changed the landscape, because 20 or 25 years ago there wasn't all of this media interactive services where people had a voice.

I think that is part of it, but I have always tried to look at stuff as being positive. I look at it as people really do care about the program. I think anytime you are in a public position there is always going to be a level of scrutiny or criticism, and there is also always going to be a level of very very high praise when things go well. Then you realize that when you are at the top you are not as good as people make you out to be, and when it is not going well you are not as bad as people make you out to be. The other thing in today's age is you have to come back to the real reason why you coach, and the real reason that I coach is because I love the game.

Coaches in my life have been some of the most influential people in my life. I hope I can help kids get prepared for the next step of their lives. With all of those things, and they are great admirable things, there is also the winning element that allows you to stay in the position you are in.

It is kind of the way it is right now, and there was a time in coaching where there was not a lot of big money or big salaries and people got into coaching for their love of the game, and that is why I got into it.

I never want to coach and lose my passion and my love for the game. There are things in the profession that can cause you to sour your love and passion for the game that you have to bring yourself back and understand the things you are talking about. The President of our United States gets criticized pretty well, and I am not comparing what we do to what he does, but I think anybody in that public spotlight, there is going

Three Gator stars from both championship runs were picked in the Top 10 of the 2007 NBA Draft - Al Horford (3), Corey Brewer (7), Joakim Noah (9).

to be a level of criticism that comes with it.

I think there is always criticism because people do care, and that doesn't mean they are accurate, doesn't mean they are right, and that doesn't mean they know what they are talking about. It is their opinion, and that is really what it comes down to. Just as when somebody says you are the greatest coach on the face of the Earth, guys don't have a problem when that is being said, but you have to take both the good and the bad.

You are only in your early 40s. What areas do you feel you need to improve upon as a coach?

Donovan: The one thing for me is that I am always eager to learn and I am always eager to get better, and I hope I am better today than I was yesterday, and hopefully I am better today than I was a year ago. I think through experiences you have a chance to grow and get better.

I want to get better in every aspect. I want to become a better coach on the floor, I want to become a better teacher, I want to become better recruiter, I want to become a better communicator, I want to become a better inspirer, I want to be a guy who shows more care.

Every facet of coaching, if you feel like you have it figured it out and "I don't need to get better", I think that is a problem. I think the one thing that is great about life is you are always in a position that you can learn, grow, and get better.

If you accept that, and often times it will take a level of humility to acknowledge that you have to get better. Some people look at that as being a weakness and I think some people want to come across like they have it all figured out.

The one thing you realize in life is that nobody has life figured out, in any aspect of it. I think keeping a level of humility and understanding of who you are and the opportunity you have been blessed with, and then going out there and trying to improve on everything that you do daily.

I mean, I want to be a better husband and I want to be a better father, I want to get better in every area of my life and that to me is exciting. I like that part of it.

Coach Donovan is one of just four in DI history to make it to the NCAA Final Four as a player, assistant and head coach.

Rick Barnes

August 8, 2007

With a 100 guesses I bet you couldn't come up with where we were able to secure some time with Coach Barnes. I'm pretty confident that if you have bothered to take 100 cracks at it you would not have put the Cracker Barrel restaurant off I-40's Exit 125 in Hickory, North Carolina, on your list.

It isn't as random as it might seem. Coach Barnes grew up in this western North Carolina city and played his college hoops for the Bears of Lenoir-Rhyne. It took a number of months to find a time that worked, and we were fortunate to have a lot of help from Leslie Parks in the UT basketball office.

As of Monday, August 6, we still were not sure if it was going to happen and time was running out. That is when my phone rang at 5:48 p.m. with Coach Barnes himself on the other end of the line. He had all of Wednesday morning available and gave me his number and said to call back when we were enroute. Unfortunately, Dave could not join me due to a death in his family.

Tuesday night, during the nine-hour drive to Hickory, I called Coach Barnes again. Knowing that I wasn't going to make it to Hickory until late that night, he asked what a good time would be for me, not for him, but for me. Pretty rare. After a few moments we settled on 9 a.m. at the Cracker Barrel.

The following morning I arrived at 8:30 and sat on the bench alone, nervously waiting for Coach Barnes to pull up. Usually it is both Dave and I, and it was strange being by myself.

The Texas coach walked up just before 9:00 and as we exchanged introductions, he requested a table for three. I was unsure of the situation and how it was going to unfold, but it ended up great. The third person turned out to be Mr. Neill McGeachy, an old friend of Coach Barnes and the current athletic director at Lenoir-Rhyne.

The three of us got to talking for better than 20 minutes before starting the interview and I felt like an old friend of the pair myself. After a

Coach Barnes lettered for three years at Lenoir-Rhyne College in Hickory, N.C., his hometown, from 1974-77. His wife, Candy, is also from Hickory.

bowl of oatmeal and about 45 minutes, Mr. McGeachy departed, leaving Coach Barnes and myself alone at the table.

Before the trip, I read a number of articles about Coach Barnes and his supposedly "egoless personality". Those articles could not have been more on the money.

We ended up talking for nearly two hours both on and off the record about a multitude of things. I really felt as though I was conversing with an old friend.

We made our way out just before 11 a.m. as Coach Barnes was headed to the Charlotte airport with his wife, Candy, to catch an early afternoon flight, but not before he told me to call him if I needed anything.

Driving down, the thought came to me that the drive home would be really horrendous if Coach Barnes was hurried for time or not a particularly good interview. It could not have gone any better than it did, and it was a great way to put a wrap on the interviewing portion of the project.

AT CLEMSON IN 1996-97, COACH BARNES LED THE TIGERS TO THE NO. 2 SPOT IN THE NATIONAL RANKINGS, THE HIGHEST IN SCHOOL HISTORY.

The gift shop area of a Crackel Barrel restaurant in Coach Barnes' hometown of Hickory, North Carolina.

Rick Barnes Profile

BORN:

July 17, 1954

HOMETOWN:

Hickory, North Carolina

HIGH SCHOOL:

Hickory

COLLEGE:

Lenoir-Rhyne - 1977

MAJOR:

Health and Physical Education

Coach Barnes was named the head coach at Texas on April 12, 1998. At the time, UT had just seven players on scholarship.

Rick Barnes Year-by-Year

Year	School	W-L (Pct.)	Postseason
1987-88	George Mason	20-10 (.667)	----
1988-89	Providence	18-11 (.621)	NCAA First Round
1989-90	Providence	17-12 (.586)	NCAA First Round
1990-91	Providence	19-13 (.594)	NIT
1991-92	Providence	14-17 (.452)	----
1992-93	Providence	20-13 (.606)	NIT
1993-94	Providence	20-10 (.667)	NCAA First Round
1994-95	Clemson	15-13 (.536)	NIT
1995-96	Clemson	18-11 (.621)	NCAA First Round
1996-97	Clemson	23-10 (.697)	NCAA Sweet Sixteen
1997-98	Clemson	18-14 (.563)	NCAA First Round
1998-99	Texas	19-13 (.594)	NCAA First Round
1999-00	Texas	24-9 (.727)	NCAA Second Round
2000-01	Texas	25-9 (.735)	NCAA First Round
2001-02	Texas	22-12 (.647)	NCAA Sweet Sixteen
2002-03	Texas	26-7 (.788)	NCAA Final Four
2003-04	Texas	25-8 (.758)	NCAA Sweet Sixteen
2004-05	Texas	20-11 (.645)	NCAA First Round
2005-06	Texas	30-7 (.811)	NCAA Elite Eight
2006-07	Texas	25-10 (.714)	NCAA Second Round
20 Seasons		**418-220 (.655)**	

Despite a short bench in 1998-99, Texas won its first outright Big XII title in school history with a record of 13-3 in conference.

Interview with Rick Barnes

What do you hope players take away from their time with you as a coach?

Barnes: I would hope that when they look back and reflect back at their time with our staff, one day I would love for them to think that it was the greatest experience of their lives - that they had a chance to grow in every area and still be able to chase their dream. Because the great thing about our job is that we get to deal with people that are chasing their dreams. That is what makes coaching what it is today, everyday you get up you are working with those who in the pursuit of a dream, and basketball is a big part of that dream.

A real disappointment would be if they looked back and said, "Coach, we wish you would have done more." So we want to make sure that the time we have with our athletes that we provide to them, help them, give them everything that they can, not only basketball-wise but that they grow as people and academically. That they look back and say, "That was an opportunity that I took great advantage of."

When you look at your coaching stops, you volunteered at Davidson and worked your way up as an assistant, then got a head job at George Mason. People talk about their "big break", what was your big break?

Barnes: First of all, I had no clue what went on in this business. I knew I wanted to coach, but I always grew up wanting to be a high school coach. When I came out of college I knew I could coach and I thought I could teach, but the only subject I had interest in teaching was health and physical education, really just physical education, but there was no jobs to be had.

Paul Abbott, a local business guy here (in Hickory), took me to the ACC tournament and when I walked out of that building I knew that day that I would like to try to get into college coaching.

We had an alumnus of Lenoir-Rhyne College who was able to set it up for me to go up to Appalachian State. I had no clue how to set up an interview. I had personally driven all over the state. I took my resume and tried to get into the offices of head coaches and say, "What can I do to get into head coaching?" Nobody gave me a concrete answer.

That day he took me up there to Appalachian State, they told me if I

Since 2000, Coach Barnes has produced three consensus All-Americans and three Top 10 NBA Draft picks - Chris Mihm, T.J. Ford and Kevin Durant.

was going to get into this business, I was going to have to volunteer or do anything that I could to get started. I made up my mind I was going to be a volunteer coach somewhere. A week or so later, it so happened that the same guy that took me to the ACC tournament was a huge North Carolina State fan. I called him and said, "Do you know Eddie Biedenbach?" He said, "I do know Eddie." So I said, "Well, do you think you could get me an interview with him?"

He called Eddie and Eddie called him back and said, "I would be glad to meet with him." Now, this story has been told many times, not always right, but it has been told. So we set up an appointment, and I went down there, and Eddie forgot the appointment.

I got up early that morning, got to Davidson really early and was waiting and waiting. I'll never forget how hot it was there, and they (the assistant coaches) never once invited me to come in that air-conditioned office, so I'm just sitting out there just burning up. I just sat there all day long, my wife even called because she was worried to death that I hadn't got back home yet.

I told her, "Well, I'm going to stay until he gets here." Finally, they (assistants) left at 5:00 p.m., and I'm still sitting there. At 7 o'clock I finally said, "I'm going to leave, and I'm coming back tomorrow."

As I get up and I'm walking down the steps, here comes Eddie and when he saw me he went, "Rick Barnes!" The thing I remember is that he had a red briefcase.

So we go upstairs and he told me, "I owe you a favor. Look, I don't know you, but why don't you work at my camp?" He handed me a bunch of brochures and said, "See if you can get some people to come to the camp." Well, I go down and work the camp for two weeks, and at the end of it he said to me, "Why don't you come down every weekend to be a volunteer?" I said, "I don't want to do that, I really want to get into this, and if you will help get me a job, I will move down here."

So he got me a job at Hope Lumber Company, so I worked there in the morning and all Eddie said to me was, "I am going to put you in charge of this camp, I want you to grow this camp and I want you to make me money."

I read about your constant "pranking". Is this a true thing? It certainly isn't something I would expect from many head coaches.

Coach Barnes led the Longhorns to their first NCAA Final Four in 56 years in 2002-03 and earned the first NCAA Tourney 1-seed in school history.

The thing I have learned is that I take my job seriously, but I don't take myself too seriously. The thing I believe is that what you do is every bit as important as what I do, so I never felt as being a coach entitled me to think that I am any better or any worse than anybody else.

I have always had a great respect for everybody in anything I do. I try to keep it light, and I try to enjoy it along the way, but also I look back at my experiences. I have been an assistant coach in the SEC, assistant in the Big Ten, I was a head coach in the ACC, a head coach in the Colonial, assistant in the Southern Conference, and now a head coach in the Big XII.

I have covered most of the power leagues and through all of this the one thing that I learned is that you never stop learning, and you are always in the learning mode. I think I would like to go back to what I said about my players looking back having a great time, I would them to look back and say it was a fun time.

I think you can have it both ways, I think you can work hard and then when it is over with I think you can turn it off and be normal people. It would really bother me if my players ever regretted coming to practice. I want people that are upbeat, people that are consistent, and I want that for my players. I love having fun.

Your 2007 recruiting class is coming in from Oregon, New Hampshire, New Jerey and Texas and you've had kids from all over. Can you talk about your take on recruiting?

Barnes: The University of Texas is a powerful place, the name speaks volumes. When I was hired I asked them, "What are you all looking for with a basketball program? Everyone knows about the great tradition of football." They said, "We want our basketball program to mirror the University of Texas."

I want it to be bigger than anything on campus, so what I am saying to you is that we want our basketball to be as big as it can be because we are willing to make that commitment. I think anybody knows you have to control your home base as much as you can, but we also feel like we have a calling card that can take us anywhere in the world - forget just the United States - we can go anywhere in the world.

I have always have had great assistants, I've always wanted to hire guys that I knew wanted to be head coaches because those are the kind

In 2006-07, freshman phenom Kevin Durant, from Suitland, Maryland, averaged 25.8 points and 11.1 rebounds for the Longhorns.

of guys that are going to invest in the work, and they know they want to have a chance to run a program, so I allow those guys to work.

One of my greatest experiences being with Eddie Beidenbach, being with Joe Harrington and Gary Williams is that they allowed me to work and they expected me to do my job. A big part of my job as an assistant coach was recruiting and they didn't limit me to where I could go. They just wanted me to get the best players and best people I could get, so I have had that kind of philosophy with my players.

Sometimes as an assistant coach, I felt that I could recruit anybody, but as a head coach you say, "Why would we recruit Kevin Durant? He is the best player in the country, certainly one of the top two players in the country, why would he leave (the Maryland area - Durant is from Suitland, MD)?"

But I have to give credit to the assistants because they did their homework and they felt if we could get him on campus that we had a shot, and that is what we did. Everybody does their little part and it is a program that you are selling not just one aspect of it. Sometimes you get lucky, sometimes it falls into your lap, but you have to work hard and put yourself into position and promote things to happen.

What was the run to the Final Four in 2003 like for you?

Barnes: We don't take for granted getting into the tournament. Getting into the tournament means you are one of 65 teams playing for the national championship.

Obviously, when you get into the Final Four you are two games away from winning the whole thing. I just remember the night we played Michigan State in San Antonio there were 32,000 people there, and I'm telling you 30,000 of them were from UT. With less than a minute to go it was obvious we were going to win the game, probably 10 or 15 seconds, and there was a foul. The guys gathered around and I remember looking at them and saying, "Hey guys, we are going to the Final Four!" That is what I remember.

Once we got to the Final Four we went about our business and we got beat by a great team and a great player that day (Syracuse's Carmelo Anthony scored 33 points and grabbed 15 rebounds in the national semi-final game as the Orange defeated Texas, 95-84). We played a great game and it wasn't like we played lousy, I mean it was a great basketball game.

Durant, a consensus All-American, won nearly every National Player of the Year award possible and was the second overall pick to the Seattle Supersonics.

Overtime: Dick Vitale & Jay Bilas
July 24, 2006 & August 5, 2006

We were fortunate to meet with a lot of great coaches through this project, but we were also fortunate to meet a lot of great people that are not coaches, but still play an integral part in representing and making the game what it is. Two of the most notable are ESPN analyst and former Duke standout Jay Bilas and the biggest fan of college hoops, the man who can't believe he gets paid to announce games, Dick Vitale, better known to some simply as "Dicky V".

If you think for a minute that Dick Vitale is putting on a show or conducting an act while he's on television, you're completely wrong. Sitting at the Broken Egg Restaurant on a hot July morning in Siesta Key, Florida, he was just as passionate about the game, if not more, for the entire two hours that we spent with him.

Sitting outside, a large number of people approached him during the time and never once did he give the people less than what they wanted. He talked hoops, he signed autographs and he took pictures with everyone who approached the table. Only once did he answer his phone and that was with regard to a charity event to benefit children. It would've been easy to be let down after having seen him so regularly on television, but we weren't in the least, he was great.

Louisville is where we met Jay Bilas, despite making his home in Charlotte, North Carolina. Having just finished a charity golf event, we met with the 1986 Blue Devil graduate in the rowdy late afternoon clubhouse at Lake Forest Country Club. A former lawyer, Jay is as sharp as they come. Like a number of coaches, our time with Jay was more of a conversation as opposed to an interview. That was in mid-August of 2006 and certainly without Jay extending his continuing help to us, we never would have been able to pull it off.

Here is a sampling of the questions that we asked during our time with Dick and Jay.

Vitale was the head coach of the Detroit Titans from 1973-77, compiling a record of 78-30.

Interview with Dick Vitale

When did you feel that broadcasting was your home?

Vitale: When it really hit is when I knew that I was connecting with the people. Initially I wanted to get back into coaching college. I thought my spirit, my energy, and my enthusiasm belonged in college more than the NBA.

But my boss, Scotty Connal, he kept telling me, "Dick, think about it because you connect, you have something that is magical with television. A lot of broadcasters, when the game is done, people don't even know who they were and could care less, but what you have within you is that when you say something, whether they agree or disagree, they respond."

What goes into a broadcast for you in terms of how much preparation?

Vitale: My prep is broken down into long-term preparation and short-term. Long term is obviously right now (in the summer). I just talked to Gary Williams, and when I get done with you guys I am going to be talking with a couple more coaches.

With Gary on Saturday I said, "Gary tell me what you know about the ACC: who looks good? Who has what coming back? What do you feel?" I talk to Tom Izzo, "What do you feel about the Big Ten? Give me a breakdown of the Big Ten. Really? Oh Wow! Wisconsin is going to be that good?"

So I do a long-term preparation and then when I have a specific assignment of two teams… I zero in. Through the internet I find articles related to those teams. Who's hot? Who's not hot? What players are on fire? What are their percentages in the last three games? What have they done on the road? What have they done at home?

I zero in between what the news media can lay on me, what the sports information directors can lay on me and ultimately, the coaches. Specifically, the assistant coaches because they are not as guarded as a lot of the head coaches, so they will tell you some things that are a little more intimate. Then I put all of that together in my game plan, and then in my mind I break down the certain weak areas and tendencies of each team. I zero in, and really put all of my emphasis on the two teams I have been assigned.

Born on June 9, 1939, Vitale joined ESPN for the 1979-80 season, shortly after the launch of the network.

Best game that you have broadcasted, watched, or one that really sticks out in your memory?

Vitale: One game - and I have had many great great games - but one that has always stood out was No. 1 versus No. 2 in the nation. Virginia and North Carolina, Ralph Sampson against Michael Jordan.

The Tar Heels were down big with about 1:50 to go and miraculously they came back and won, and it was just phenomenal to see how Jordan performed even at a young age under pressure.

Then obviously, all the Duke and Carolina games over the years have been so special. I have done 30 or 40 of those games and they have been so great. Just be a little part of that whole environment has been so special.

A GREAT FRIEND OF THE LATE JIM VALVANO, VITALE IS ON THE V FOUNDATION BOARD OF DIRECTORS.

At the Broken Egg restaurant on Siesta Key, Florida near Sarasota. Mr. Vitale had already appeared on ESPN Radio, played tennis and read a large stack of newspapers by the time we met with him around 9:30 a.m.

Outside the clubhouse at Lake Forest Country Club near Louisville, Kentucky. Jay had taken part in a golf tournament earlier in the day with his brother.

At Rolling Hills High School in Southern California, Bilas averaged 23.7 points and 13.5 rebounds as a senior.

Interview with Jay Bilas

When you chose Duke back in '82 it was just becoming a premier program, what made you take that step from California?

Bilas: I really liked Coach K a lot, I had not heard of him before he started recruiting me, but I just felt comfortable. I wanted to play for a coach who I trusted. Who I played for was more important than where I played.

I felt like I could get a great education at a lot of places and Duke was one of them. I narrowed it down to three coaches: Jim Boeheim, Lute Olson, and Coach K. You can only choose one, and I chose Coach K. It was a good decision for me - and you can't go wrong with any of those guys - but it worked out really well for me and I played with some really great guys, and had a great relationship with Coach K.

What kind of preparation goes into a story, or the NBA draft, etc?

Bilas: I do it all the time and I don't feel like I am ever cramming for anything. During the year I watch tape a lot and I watch games all the time. I will watch tape of a half here and a half there and there is not a day that goes by during the year that I don't watch basketball.

I watch international basketball, I watch college, I watch pro, I take notes while I'm watching and keep it in a book so if I have the team later on, I have it already. I do the standard stuff, I talk on the phone to a lot to coaches, and if I am not covering them for a couple more months I try to at least keep tabs on teams, teams that I think are going to be good.

I can't say that I am watching the bottom two teams in every league, but if the team is competitive, I'm watching it, and I may watch if I think they will be competitive in the next year.

How do you split time with being a lawyer and the basketball?

Bilas: I don't anymore, I used to, from 1993-2000 I was full time lawyer. Then it became too difficult, and my wife said, "You have to choose. It doesn't matter what you do, but you have to choose." She was right because I was gone all the time, and when I was home I was always in the office and I just couldn't do it anymore, and I figured I could always get back into law if I want to.

Bilas graduated from Duke in '86 with a degree in Political Science. After playing professionally overseas, Jay graduated from Duke Law School in '92.

What do you like most about your analyst job with ESPN?

Bilas: I like the whole process, I like going to practices, and I like watching film and watching film with coaches and all that stuff. Most coaches are kind enough to let me in and watch practices and go to their meetings. I have never been turned down by anybody to watch a practice, and it has been a nice time.

I have learned a lot about the game. I was brought up in the game in a certain way and I have learned a lot from the coaches I have been around. How they do it has changed the way I look at things.

We went to ESPN last year...what is the atmosphere at ESPN through your eyes?

Bilas: It's like a college in many ways, active 24 hours a day, and hard to find a parking spot. It's a great place to work because everybody cares about what they are doing, they care about the product they put on the air, and they care about the sports. They care about doing a good job. It is a really fun place, and most of the people there are younger, so it is kind of fun being around the younger folk.

The only downside is when I am up there I am away from my home. You are away from your family for long periods of time and that gets old after awhile. That is ultimately what will get me out of this. I will ultimately quit doing this at some point because I am away too much, and that is going to weigh on me at some point. As much as I love going to basketball games, and I love it, I like hanging out with my family more.

Bilas is a partner in the charitable foundation Athletes United for Youth which benefits youth education in the greater Charlotte area.

The Final Buzzer

Wow! What a 15-month ride. There were so many times Dave and I would laugh and shake our heads in disbelief as we were spending time with one coach after the next, turning our idea into a reality.

At first, the goal of sitting down with the NCAA's greatest seemed far fetched, outlandish and even a bit crazy. However, with the cooperation and assistance of the sports information directors, secretaries, assistants and the coaches themselves, slowly but surely, everything came to fruition.

Any one of the coaches involved easily could've said, "Thanks, but no thanks" and that would've been the end of the line - that's the most amazing thing to us. Instead, despite insane schedules and time constraints, they were enthusiastic and optimistic about our journey, and many went so far to genuinely offer their help and assistance to us in the future.

Before we started this project, we knew that college basketball was a unique sport, but we had no idea of the overwhelmingly giving and generous attitudes possessed by the leaders and caretakers of the game.

A great compliment in our eyes came from Hall of Famer John Chaney. Following our interview in Atlanta at the Final Four, an internet based news source, who was doing a story on *Destination Basketball,* asked Coach Chaney about his experience with us. He responded by saying, "It is more of a human kind of interview where the question touches you a little bit more, and it gives you a relaxing feeling when you are able to talk about some of your experiences."

When we heard this, we knew that our mission had been accomplished with at least one coach. Hopefully a number of others felt the same when we parted ways, even if only for a moment.

Whether you are a fan of the game or not, we hope that you have been able to learn something about the 29 teachers involved in this book. Teachers are some of the greatest and most influential people in the world, and while the people involved with *Destination Basketball* are coaches by title, they are teachers by trade.

Despite different styles, backgrounds and philosophies, they are all trying to accomplish the same thing - to help shape the lives of young individuals from around the world become the best that they can be as players and the best that they can be as people.